Ricksha Days

Remembering Shanghai

Leta Tucker Hodge

Published by
AKA-Publishing
Columbia, MO 65203

Trade Paperback ISBN 978-1-936688-66-1

Also available in Dust jacketed Hardback ISBN 978-1-936688-71-5

Compass Flower Press
an imprint of AKA-Publishing

Ricksha Days

Remembering Shanghai

Leta Tucker Hodge

Shanghai

Points of Interest

1. The Grosvenor House
2. Cathay Mansions
3. Shanghai American School
4. Community Church
5. Cavendish Court
6. Columbia Country Club
7. Pootung Camp
8. BAT Thornburn Roads Factory

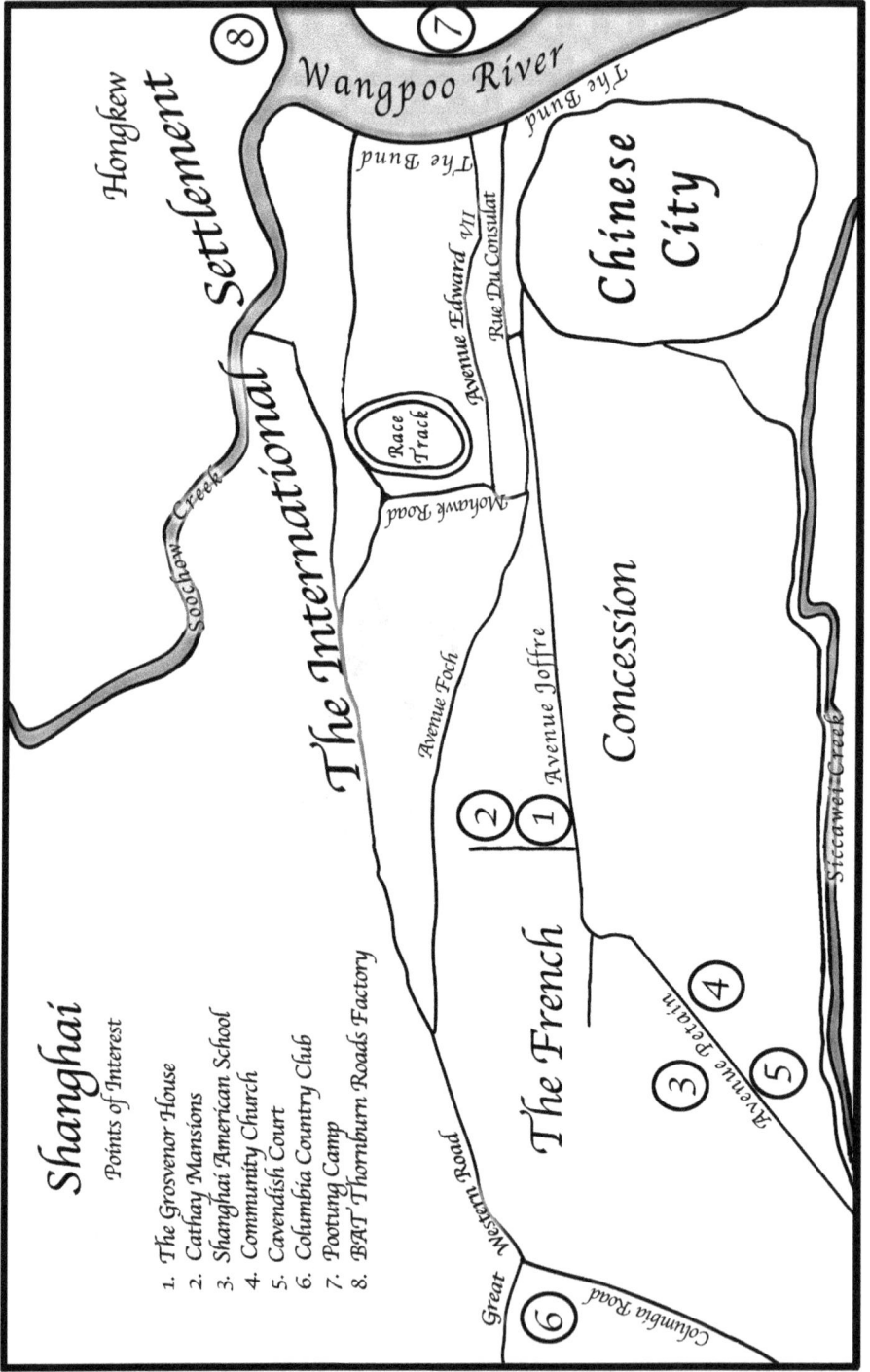

Hongkew

Settlement

The International

Wangpoo River

⑧

⑦

The Bund

The Bund

Rue Du Consulat

Avenue Edward VII

Chinese City

Race Track

Mohawk Road

Soochow Creek

Avenue Foch

Avenue Joffre

②

①

Concession

The French

Avenue Petain

③

④

⑤

Siccawei Creek

Great Western Road

Columbia Road

⑥

For my Grandchildren

Jacob
Adam
Matthew
Maxwell
Hanna

Also by the author:

A Gathering of Our Days: Selected Writings on the History of Mexico and Audrain County

Soldiers, Scholars, Gentlemen: The First Hundred Years of the Missouri Military Academy

The Friend of Audrain: A History of Medicine in Audrain County, Missouri

Contents

Book Three

2

Foreword

My "ricksha days" did not last long, as these things go. I lived in China from my birth in 1934 until 1940, and again from 1946 until December of 1948. My life during those years was profoundly affected by China, by Shanghai and by the society symbolized by the ricksha.

These days saw war, death and destruction—not only of people and material things but of the whole culture into which I was born. They reflected a way of life—in many ways an unusual and lovely way of life for those of us living it—that disappeared during the years of my childhood. Wars and change overwhelmed it all. Even the ricksha could not survive as it was and gradually gave way to the modern. The society that my parents and I knew was crushed and eventually gave way to Mao Tse Tung and his communist regime. Little survived of my early years and the kind of life I lived.

Because I think it is important to understand one's past and the people from whom we are descended, I have attempted to record the story of my life in China, at least the way that I remember it, for

3

those who come after me. I have relied not only on my memories—limited, since I was just a child—but also on stories, letters, diaries, newspaper accounts and other records left by my parents. As an academic historian I have done extensive reading to better grasp the events that were taking place around me. The memories, though, are my own and I have chosen to stick very close to them.

Perhaps this effort will provide some insight into the Americans—and the children—once calling China home. We viewed Shanghai—the good and the bad—with unceasing fascination. And we remember with mixed feelings that small slice of her past we came to call the ricksha days.

Prologue:
Once Again, Shanghai

The waters of the Yangtze River, murky and menacing, streamed toward the China Sea, sliding around us and slapping at the sides of the *SS Marchen Maersk* where I stood on deck. No longer did the blazing summer sun shine on blue Pacific waves; now it bore down on yellow-brown river water spreading to the hazy horizon. Lying at anchor, engines cut back, idly drifting in the middle of this giant, steaming mud puddle, we were waiting for permission to proceed up river to Shanghai.

It was Monday afternoon, September 2, 1946. My mother, my brother Bill and I had been on this small Danish freighter for the past thirty-four days. Celebrating my twelfth birthday had been one of the few highlights of the long tedious trip from Virginia through the Panama Canal, up the west coast to California and across the Pacific Ocean to China. Along with the nine other passengers, we were bored with the daily routine, eager for land and impatient for journey's end.

The previous night I had written in my diary: "Had last dinner

(I hope) on this ship." But as the hours inched by, disappointment replaced excitement as we realized there would be no landing today. We were in for one more dinner and one more hot, restless night. When a river pilot boarded ship that evening, the captain announced that "early tomorrow" we would once again be moving.

The next morning before six we were underway, slowly maneuvering up the Yangtze to a place called Woosung. By nine we had dropped anchor in midstream, taking our place in a line of ships awaiting further instructions. Ahead of us, to the left, emptied the Whangpoo. It would be up this river that we would sail the remaining fourteen miles of our long voyage.

Around us crowded ships of every kind—freighters, steamers, tenders, jetties, launches, oil tankers, coal barges, an old ocean liner, sampans, Chinese junks. . . From their masts flew flags from around the world. Some I could easily identify—American, British, Russian—but others I didn't know. Waves of sound drifted across our deck: shrill whistles, resounding gongs, deep gutteral warning horns and loud voices in languages garbled and foreign. A dank salty rotting smell saturated the air. It was hard to breathe in the heavy humidity and stifling heat.

The heat was the worst we had experienced at any time on the trip. The ship in motion early this morning had been pleasant enough for sightseeing, but when it stopped and lay still beneath the sun, it became almost unbearable on deck. My feet felt scorched in their flimsy white sandals and we dared not touch the deck's metal railings. At the captain's invitation Bill and I moved up to his small, covered upper deck, grateful for the slight protection it offered. To go inside the lounge or a stuffy cabin was unthinkable. We were caught up in the activity and commotion, the excitement and mystery of this strange river.

I was such a long, long way from America.

Time dragged. The hands of my new watch barely moved. Would we never get off this ship?

At noon, as we were sitting down to cold meat sandwiches in the dining room, a launch pulled alongside bearing the ship's official Chinese agents—and my father. He had been invited to join them on the trip down to Woosung, since not only was his family on board but also, down in the hold, a large shipment of tobacco in hogsheads stenciled "W.J. Tucker, Thorburn Roads, Shanghai."

We were overjoyed to see him. It had been, this time, almost a year since he had left us in the States at the end of the war. My mother's relief at turning over all worries to him was obvious. Equally strong was my own relief at no longer bearing sole responsibility for my mother.

Through the BAT—the British American Tobacco Company for which he worked—my father had arranged for a tender to meet us downriver to carry us the rest of the way up the Whangpoo to Shanghai. It soon arrived, bobbing up and down beside the freighter. Several other passengers joined us and after our baggage was transferred we crept down the swaying gangplank to its deck. Hot and crowded, we started out. As my mother later wrote, "up the river we put, bidding farewell to the *Marchen Maersk* with no regrets."

It took some time to thread our way among the boats jamming the mouth of the river. The Whangpoo was smaller than the Yangtze and we could easily see land along each side. Flat green fields bordered its banks. Small bamboo huts stood off in the distance; in front of some, children played. Peasants in broad, round straw hats bent over rice paddies. Here and there one or two oxen, stolid and steady, plodded through shallow water, pulling low carts. Gangs of coolies, chanting as they strained at ropes, dragged loaded barges up the river.

At Pootung, where my father had been interned by the Japanese, we made a wide turn into the harbor. Across the water in front of us, glittering in the sunshine, lay Shanghai. A line of solid, European style buildings of marble, stone and granite curved along the riverfront—the Shanghai Bund. Our tender sputtered to a stop at a customs pier. It was, my mother remarked, the exact spot from which we had left six years earlier.

Trunks, boxes, suitcases and one large khaki duffel bag now had to pass through customs. Our small radio was taken to be registered; it would be returned in a few days. All of my mother's nylon stockings had to be unearthed and counted lest they be intended for the black market, but they posed no problem and none were taken. Contents of the duffel bag were removed and when the inspector turned his back for a second an alert coolie passing by ran off with all he could carry, including volume 3-4 of our Book of Knowledge set. There was much discussion, in Chinese, about our Chevrolet, still strapped down on the main deck of the ship, but we were assured that it would be ready for us "in one week." Finally completing his task, the customs officer, charging no duty, allowed us to pass into the city.

Daddy's uniformed chauffeur stood waiting for us beside a black 1930s-style company car, every inch of which he had brushed and polished to perfection. In we got, glad for an end to the official part of our arrival, but still miserable in the heat. It was, we were told, the fourteenth day of an unprecedented heat wave. Inside the car, with all windows down, a hot breeze stirred, bringing with it smells of the city: sewage and garbage rotting in the river, oil and gas fumes rising from a massive traffic snarl, and food cooking in stalls along the piers. A dozen or more coolies, shouting, waving their arms and hawking their wares, pressed around the car. Everywhere I looked were swarms of people.

We set out at once for the Grosvenor House. The chauffeur, constantly blowing the car horn, pulled slowly out into the Bund. Clearing a path through the automobiles and street cars, rickshas, pedicabs, bicycles, wheelbarrows, carts and throngs of human beings, he plowed steadily on toward Avenue Edward VII. At last we turned into the quieter streets of the old French Concession.

In less than a half hour we had passed the Chinese guard at the gate to the Grosvenor House compound and the doorman was opening the car doors for us at the broad steps of the main entrance. The tall imposing granite and red brick building towered over me as it always had. Tired but excited, we entered the large bright white marble foyer. The Chinese elevator boy in his customary long gray gown greeted my father first and then welcomed us in broken English and ushered us into his lift.

Two minutes later we were filing into the foyer of Apartment 303. With its familiar muffled little sigh the heavy front door closed once more behind me. Waiting inside the hall stood our faithful Amah.

"Wer-come back, Missy," she said to my mother, smiling and bowing.

Then, her black eyes shining and a wide grin revealing her gold tooth, she was reaching out to Bill and me, taking our hands and admiring how much we had grown. I was glad to see her. But at the same time I felt myself puzzled and strangely angry at this tiny, black-haired woman, remembering vaguely that once—long ago—she somehow had deserted me.

The apartment was cool, the light soft and the air much more comfortable. Ceiling fans droned above us. Some of our old furniture, carefully spruced up, was visible here and there. Vases of flowers, arranged by Amah, stood in the living room, dining room and veranda. Everything looked spotless. No carved wooden junk reigned on the living room mantle, but in its same old place sat the picture of Mama, Bill and me. Things seemed more and more familiar as I looked around me. My mother wandered about touching everything. Her eyes lighting up like I had rarely seen them, she was clearly coming home.

Virginia was so far, far away.

Our Chinese "No. 1 Boy," called "Boy" and new to us, announced dinner at six-thirty and we sat down together at our own dining room table. It was meticulously set, even to the finger bowls, with borrowed blue and white china monogrammed YTT—Yee Tsoong Tobacco Company, Daddy's branch of the BAT. Boy and Amah proudly served us a delicious dinner of fried chicken, rice, green peas and apple pie. We relished every morsel.

Well before nine o'clock I was ready for bed. Bill's "bedroom" had been set up at the end of the veranda, so now I had the large former nursery to myself. There was little in this sparsely furnished room that looked familiar. Where now were my cherished dolls that once had filled the shelves beneath the windows?

Amah had already laid out my freshly laundered pajamas, turned down the sheet and unfurled the filmy white mosquito net suspended from the ceiling. I slipped under the net, careful to tuck it in again, and lay back on an immaculate linen pillow. Everything smelled of soap, hot iron and camphorwood. I smiled in appreciation.

In my mind I knew that this was home—the only real home I had ever known. It was good to be back. In my heart, though, I faltered. I wondered if I would ever again feel at home here, if I even wanted to feel at home here. But my father's job was here. For more than twenty years his life had been tied directly to China. And so, of course, was mine.

I was tired and quickly fell asleep, only dimly aware of distant traffic and Chinese voices now and then drifting up to my windows from the compound below—sounds once so familiar.

We had, indeed, come back. In spite of everything—all those years, all that waiting, all that worry—I was here again. Despite the past, and whatever the days ahead might bring, it was, once again, Shanghai.

Book One

China Calling

China, in the 1920s, was about as far away as a young man could get from the tobacco fields of southern Virginia. For my father, Jake Tucker, plowing and planting those tobacco fields, the opportunities to build a satisfying life seemed limited, if not absent. Because China beckoned and because he had the courage to take a chance, he changed the course of his life—and, of course, the lives of his children.

He was born in Gold Leaf, Virginia on June 28, 1896 and named William Jacob Tucker after his father. The American people were about to elect William McKinley president, the Spanish-American War lay just over the horizon and Teddy Roosevelt would soon become a national hero. Telephones and electricity were changing everyday life and the approaching new century would bring with it the automobile, movies, radio, the airplane and countless other wonders.

Gold Leaf and the nearby Palmer Springs area were to be my father's home for twenty-five years. Located in Mecklenburg

County, in the southern piedmont region of Virginia, not far from the North Carolina line, Gold Leaf was a small community centered around little more than a store and a post office. It was tobacco growing country. The name itself was a reminder of the golden color of tobacco leaves at harvest time and of the wealth inherent in the crop that had for nearly three hundred years been the mainstay of Virginia's economy—the leaf valued as gold.

In Gold Leaf Jake's father, William Jacob Tucker, Sr., ran the general store and farmed some land. In 1886, at age thirty-one, he had married Miss Susan Margaret Park, of a large Mecklenburg family. They had eight children: three boys and five girls—all fair-haired and blue-eyed. Jake was in the middle, the second of the boys. They lived in a two-story white frame house next to the store. For years, while the children were little, his mother ran the post office located in their store. Not too far away lived a host of relatives, from aunts and uncles to first cousins, second cousins, kissing cousins, cousins by marriage, cousins once removed and cousins twice and thrice removed.

The Civil War, or War Between the States as they called it, only thirty years in the past, was still a powerful presence in Gold Leaf, even for children like Jake. On the Tucker side of the family this war had cost him two grandparents, making an orphan of his father. John Daniel Tucker, Jake's grandfather, had enlisted as a private in the Confederate Army, where he saw action at Chickamauga, among other places. In 1864 he, like so many other Confederate soldiers, caught the measles—or "the plague"—and died. His personal effects, including his uniform, were sent home to his wife, Frances, who opened the box, handled the contents and caught the disease herself. Within days she, too, had died, leaving their five children to be raised by relatives. Years later Frances's son William would name his first daughter in her memory, calling her Fannie; she was Jake's oldest sister.

On his mother's side of the family this war had also left its mark. Jake frequently saw her father, his other grandfather, Thomas Adams Park. He had volunteered in 1861, at the age of twenty, and left home with the Clarksville (Va.) Blues; later he became a part of Company E, 14ᵗʰ Virginia Regiment, C.S.A. At least three of his brothers served in the Confederate Army. Before they left home their mother, Margaret, told them that for as long as the war lasted they should know that every day, rain or shine, at sundown she would be at their nearby church, praying for them. For the rest of her life she was called "with great affection," by family and friends alike, "Praying Peggy." Her sons saw some of the worst fighting of the war, including Gettysburg, where one "left an arm" and Tom was taken prisoner. All survived. Even a young boy like Jake could see at first hand the distress and despair—as well as the pride—that this war still sparked in his family and those around him.

Along with the other children, Jake attended the nearby rural school. His education stressed reading, writing and ciphering, with some history and geography. He always spoke correct English, thanks probably to his mother's example, with a Virginia accent but none of the common lapses in grammar that marked many of his contemporaries. At the end of eighth grade, the limit of most rural schools, his formal education stopped. He spent his time from then on at his father's store and in the tobacco fields.

At the age of twenty-two, with the nation caught up in World War I, Jake Tucker enlisted in the army and was sent to Fort Benning, Georgia, for basic training. His stay, however, was short, since Armistice Day in November, 1918 ended the war, releasing him from further service. Formal photographs taken then show a solemn young man of average build with blond hair. His friends knew him as gregarious and outgoing. He never met a stranger and, being a Tucker, was always ready for a good time.

His older brother Tom had also served in the army and when the two returned home they went back to work on the family farm. Tom now began to farm as well for older relatives; Jake may have done the same. They both soon realized that, though neither was married, this kind of farming was not going to be enough to support them.

This was a typical situation for many families in those days, in that place. Times were poor and for many, prospects even poorer. Tobacco crops were wearing out the fields. By the 1920s, although new machinery was available and new methods of farming successful, few could afford them or were inclined to make changes. Many young men were leaving family farms, moving to cities and seeking different work.

For Jake Tucker, 26 years old in 1922, things were no different. By then his three older sisters, Fannie, Mamie and Willie, had married farmers and would remain in the area. His younger brother Albert had moved to Washington, D.C. and with the help of relatives had found a job. His sister Rosa, unmarried, did the same. Within a few years, his father and mother, Tom and another sister, Bertha, would join them in Washington.

In the meantime he pondered his own future. A first cousin had left home before the war to work for a major tobacco company in China. Over the next few years several distant relatives, near his age, had joined the same company. Their experiences—and particularly their improved financial status—were duly reported back home.

This company continued to seek young men knowledgeable in tobacco farming. Now, Jake, too, was ready to hear what they had to offer, realizing that his one field of expertise lay in the planting, raising and curing of Virginia tobacco. The prospects of a secure financial position and a chance for advancement helped make up his mind. His sense of adventure and desire to see the world, fueled, no doubt, by the extraordinary accounts relayed by his China cousins, clinched the decision. At the next opportunity he applied for a job and the British American Tobacco Company hired him "to teach the Chinese how to grow tobacco."

Jake began making plans to leave family, farm and Gold Leaf. Joining a group of company recruits, he headed by train for the west coast. They were booked to sail in July on a ship bound for the Orient.

On the train out of Chicago, however, the young man from Virginia became ill. Finally diagnosed with appendicitis, he was taken off the train at Helena, Montana and sent to the local hospital. Here he was operated on and stayed for "a week or two" recuperating. It was a bleak time for a country boy who knew no one. Later he would confess to being "slightly homesick," but he stuck it out. When the doctor released him, he caught the next train west and was able to rejoin the original group. He sailed with them on the assigned ship.

On August 11, 1923 William Jacob Tucker, JR. landed in Shanghai, China.

A Bachelor in China

For Jake Tucker China proved to be a fascinating place to work. The British American Tobacco Company—the BAT—was one of the largest and most prestigious firms in the Far East. One stationery letter-head reveals something of its position: *British Cigarette Company, Limited. (Incorporated under the companies ordinances of HongKong.) Head Office: Shanghai. Other main offices in Hankow and Tientsin."* For a rising young newcomer it offered status and the opportunity to make a substantial living from the China market for tobacco and cigarettes.

Like most of the men from Virginia and North Carolina, Jake was sent initially to Manchuria in north China. Efforts to grow tobacco were successful here: the land and weather were suited to the crop and the coolie population amenable to working with it. His first assignments were to such cities as Harbin, Dairen and Mukden, way to the north near Russia. Later he would be transferred to Tientsin and Tsingtao, on the China seacoast. Far from toiling in the tobacco fields himself, his job was to direct the head Chinese under him, who oversaw the actual planting, growing, picking and curing. Expected of him were instruction, advice, organization, inspection of fields and properly cured tobacco leaves. Gradually he also learned the role of manager for such a plant.

For Jake Tucker his new bachelor existence proved to be an exciting and different way of life. The Company, knowing the difficulties in sending young men, particularly Americans, to more isolated sections of China, paid them well, with generous perquisites. Otherwise the lonely conditions might have sent many of them back home.

The living conditions usually consisted of a company apartment or house, well furnished, to be shared with one or two other company men. They were waited on by Chinese servants, including a head cook, one or two coolies to see to their laundry and keep the house clean, and sometimes a gardener. These young bachelors could well afford good food, good liquor and such diversions as golf, bridge, poker and baseball. Since some owned automobiles they took trips to nearby cities and, despite the lack of good roads, throughout the countryside, vacationing often at the seashore. Typical of most British and American businessmen then living in China, they led a life style of leisure and comfort, with a visible abyss between the foreigners and the Chinese.

Few letters have survived from these early years Jake spent in China. That he was writing home steadily to his mother is apparent from the two that remain. Apparent, too, is the growing significance of Japan and the problems the Japanese were beginning to pose for China.

Japan had recently unofficially taken over portions of Manchuria, particularly along the main east-west railroad, and was sending more and more troops into the region. The most powerful Chinese warlord in the area, an authority in his own right, was a man named Chang Tso Lin, who was walking a tight line between the Japanese Army and the Chinese government while trying to maintain his own control of north China. With all the trappings of a powerful warlord Chang was occasionally seen by the public, including foreign businessmen, and was the subject of some conjecture as to his future.

On a day in the spring of 1928, Chang left Peking by train to return to Manchuria, accompanied, as usual, by a small army of close guards. When they approached a bridge near Mukden a huge explosion rocked the train, killing everyone on board—and thus doing away with a major barrier to Japanese control of Manchuria. The following letter from Jake to his mother mentions this event, of great interest to him since he was then in Mukden and recently had seen Chang. It also reveals something of the Japanese activities that eventually would lead to the Second World War.

Dear Ma,   *June 12th, 1928*

Since writing to you last things have settled down to normal again or practically so. The question that is being asked all over China is, is Chang Tso Lin dead or alive. No one seems to know definitely...

I think he is as dead as he will ever die if he was on the train and there seems to be no doubt about that. You probably don't care a rap whether he is dead or alive but I thought you might be interested in knowing just what a tangle the explosion caused.

The Japs claim that they knew nothing of the bomb being placed on the track. Very strange that all of their guards who patrol across the bridge day and night are still alive and uninjured...

It is beginning to get warm here. Feels like summer which suits me fine. The Ford is running fine and I am thoroughly enjoying it. Wouldn't be without it. . .

Hope Tom has good prospects for a crop. Haven't heard from you for some time. . .

With love to all of you, I am
Your devoted son, Jake

The other remaining letter, written barely a month later, says nothing about the political situation. He does mention a trip with company officials to Dairen, where they were entertained by some Japanese who invited them to dinner, serving, among other rare delicacies, eel—which he ate but didn't like. Emphasis is on golf and questions regarding the family.

. . .I had a letter from you recently... Hope Albert has another job before this. . . . How's Pa. I know he enjoyed riding around with Albert [in his new car]. *Would like to be there and have a few old Virginia cheroots with him. . .*

And there was this comment about his state of mind:

You mentioned that you would like for me to be home sometimes. I often wish I could be there too and sometimes get homesick, but we can't have everything just as we want it.

Home leave for the China men in the BAT came every four years. He had already returned to Virginia for his first five-month vacation in 1927. With matrimony on his mind, he began courting a young school teacher named Evelyn Harrison. He would later say that of course she was impressed by him, but she always wound up wailing that "China is so far away. . ."

Four years later on leave in the spring of 1931, it was a different story. This time he swept her off her feet and out of the schoolroom.

The School Teacher

In the spring of 1931 Evelyn Byrd Harrison was twenty-five years old, with dark hair worn fashionably close to her head, large hazel eyes, an olive complexion and a pretty smile. With a slender figure, she had a stylish look about her. She knew how to play bridge, liked to dance and loved to go to the movies.

She had a wide circle of friends, one of whom was Lucy Katherine Tucker of Palmer Springs, who had a cousin named Jake. Evelyn had already met this blond young businessman with the piercing blue eyes when he was on home leave in 1927. Although the two seemed to like each other, he had gone back to China alone. She had been left with mixed feelings about Jake Tucker.

Now Jake was back in Virginia, on leave again. When he got in touch with her Evelyn agreed to see him. And for the next two months family, friends and relatives stood back and watched what she herself called "a stormy courtship."

The young Miss Harrison was just completing her third year as an elementary school teacher. After receiving a teaching certificate from Farmville State Teacher's College, she had accepted a position at the public school in Zebulon, North Carolina—not too far from home. Friends had done the same and the three young women boarded at a house near the school. In the summers she had taken courses toward a degree from the University of North Carolina. Since her mother was a teacher, and her older sister, teaching seemed to be the path her future life would take. A love of teaching did not, however, appear to be an overwhelming passion in her life.

Born in Austell, Georgia, Evelyn had spent most of her life in La Crosse in Mecklenburg County, Virginia. This small town reflected the continuing difficult times in Virginia and the South; no one had much money. Here and in the next county lived many of her mother's relatives: Bowens and Matthews, Tanners and Evans and Braceys. Here, too, people well remembered the War Between the States and still felt the economic and emotional losses it had brought.

Evelyn's father, David Holmes Conrad Harrison, born in 1853, had been directly affected by that war. Holmes's father, George Fisher Harrison, had served in the Confederate Army all four years and when Holmes's mother died during that period, he and his sisters were raised by relatives. Two of his mother's brothers, Holmes and Tucker Conrad, alumni of the University of Virginia, had lost their lives in a single Union volley at the Battle of First Manassas—a part of General Jackson's immovable "stone wall." Another uncle was head surgeon at Richmond's main military hospital and numerous cousins served in the army.

After the war the family as a whole, once wealthy and among the state's leading citizens, faced severe financial problems. Knowing he would not be able to attend college, as would have been expected in the past, Holmes, at the age of seventeen, accepted a job with one of the railroad companies then rebuilding old lines and expanding into new areas throughout the South. He did the work of a civil engineer and though self-taught, was well regarded by his superiors. After his first wife died, leaving him with two daughters, Amelia and Rebecca, he married, in 1896, Miss Leta May Bowen of Bracey, Virginia. They had five children. The youngest, born in July, 1905, was Evelyn or, as the family called her, "Polly."

Around the time she was ready for school, Evelyn's father left the railroad, which demanded frequent moves, and the family settled at La Crosse, where he became postmaster. Her mother helped out in the post office and for many years taught school. They lived in a two-story frame house at the edge of the village. Just up the street in their new house lived her half-sister Beck and her new husband Jim Matthews. Beyond them lived her mother's sister Alta with her family.

By 1931 Evelyn's brother Thornton, already married with children, was working as manager of a large nearby estate, her brother Holmes was entering the insurance field in Richmond and her sister Nancy had for some years been teaching in Roanoke. For Evelyn, life seemed bound by family, teaching, concern for her mother, widowed in 1926, and a simple uncomplicated social scene. There would be few opportunities, she knew, for financial improvement, cultural pursuits or travel.

But when Jake Tucker appeared on the scene again, things changed. Now she was well past her adored father's death, all too fresh four years earlier. Her life suddenly opened to the possibility of seeing the world, meeting new people, living in a foreign country, enjoying some of the finer things of life—and being treated like a queen. He did indeed sweep her off her feet and she fell in love.

By the middle of June Jake had persuaded her to marry him.

China, he assured her, was a great place to live and not all that far away. The wedding date was set, first for her birthday, July 8, but then because time was short, for July 2.

They were married, my parents, on a beautiful summer afternoon in the garden at her sister Beck's home, beneath the rose arbor amid a profusion of flowers.

Dancing Under the Stars

*E*arly on the morning of July 9, 1931, the new Mr. and Mrs. W.J. Tucker, Jr., drove out of La Crosse—destination: Shanghai, China.

A number of relatives gathered to see them off, most caught up in the excitement of such a marvelous trip. It was still amazing to think that "their little Polly" was traveling half way around the world to make her home in China. Some expressed dismay at her being so far away for four years but, they reassured the bride, it would go quicker than she thought. Her grandmother, then in her eighties, was convinced that she would never lay eyes on her granddaughter again—and said so. Finally, amid a flurry of hugs and tears, the groom firmly closed the car doors and started down the road—the first leg of a long, long journey and the beginning of a storybook honeymoon.

They headed west across the state to West Virginia, spending the first night in Lewisburg. In her diary, begun on the day of her wedding, she noted "Felt terribly blue and homesick. . ."

The groom's carefully planned itinerary took them the next day to Cincinnati where they stopped for the night, then along Route 40 to Vandalia, Illinois. Averaging around 300 miles a day, they proceeded to Odessa, Missouri where they stopped early because of a storm, and the next day to Salina, Kansas. Rising at 4:30 the next morning they made the 318 miles to Syracuse, Kansas. "Hot! Hot!" reads that day's diary entry.

The young couple then drove through Colorado to Santa Fe, New Mexico. "Spent night at the 'LaFonda,' a beautiful hotel. . . I like New Mexico. Saw two real cowboys today. . ." July 17 found them in Winslow, Arizona; from there they crossed the Painted Desert to the Grand Canyon, where they spent the night. "Room didn't cost us but $14!!" she noted [a high cost]. The next day they made it through the heat to Kingman, and the following day started across the desert before dawn only to have a "puncture" delay them until after noon; this made for a miserable drive through the heat. The next morning they reached Los Angeles. After spending time sightseeing by bus, they toured Hollywood, then had a special dinner and went to a show.

On July 22 they pulled up to the St. Francis Hotel in San Francisco—the last part of the "motoring leg" of the trip. Thursday they spent shopping, buying clothes for her and gifts for her mother and Nancy, which she mailed home.

The next day they packed and got ready to board ship in the afternoon. They were booked, first class, by the "Dollar Steamship Line (Orient and Around the World)" on the *S.S. President Harrison*. She described their departure in a letter to her mother:

> *We came on board about 2:30 Friday. I wore my new outfit*
> *I bought and Jake had on a new suit so we looked quite the*

berries. We sent your telegram five minutes before we sailed in the midst of much excitement. When the ship moved off the orchestra played "Bye-Bye Blues" (of all pieces to play). Everybody threw streamers to their friends who were there to see them off. We threw them, too, even though we knew no one.

Then we gathered on deck and had tea—hot, of course. I never did like it. Just about the time we got through the Golden Gate we ran into a storm. . . .We went into our cabin and got all settled. Jake had bought me six or eight magazines and a big box of candy and we found on the dresser a telegram from the Covingtons sending their best wishes.

But the sea was getting rougher & rougher and I was getting sicker & sicker. We just rocked and reeled and swayed around like a rubber ball would have, and I was so sick. I couldn't pretend to sit up. . . There were about forty who couldn't go to dinner that night. . . I stayed in bed all of Saturday, but yesterday I made myself get up for a while in the morning and again for dinner last night.

The sea finally calmed down, becoming very smooth. "To look four ways and see nothing but water," wrote the unseasoned traveler, "gives you a kinder funny feeling if you stop to think about it. I don't stop."

Their days were spent reading out on deck, writing letters home, and playing shuffleboard, bridge and "Horse Races," a gambling game at which she played three or four times and lost. At their assigned table in the dining room were a young naval officer and his wife from Kentucky, also going to Shanghai, who often joined them for various activities.

The evenings offered spectacular dinners, the latest movies and dancing under the stars. One diary entry reads: "Last night we danced for an hour or so out on deck. The moon was shining and the orchestra was good. . ."

Early on the last day of July the ship docked in Honolulu. They took a taxi and rode around the island, shopped for a while, had lunch and then walked up Waikiki Beach to the Royal Hawaiian Hotel. He bought her a "real cute pair of beach pajamas in a little shop in the hotel. They are white with big red dots on them." Another big thrill—and here she reflected the impact of the relatively new medium of motion pictures on society as a whole—was sitting near the beach and seeing two movie stars, William Powell and his new bride, Carole Lombard. She seemed impressed by him, not too taken with her.

The ship sailed at six. "For about an hour before we left there were about twenty native boys in the water around the ship, diving for money. The passengers would throw pieces over. I think Jake threw about seventy-five cents in nickels. . ."

By Tuesday they were suffering from the heat, anticipating that by the time they reached China "we will be burning down." Evelyn was given a smallpox vaccination, a necessary procedure they had not had time for earlier; she later noted that it did not take.

On their one month anniversary Jake arranged for the orchestra to play at dinner that night "I Love You Truly" and "Indian Love Call," both sung at their wedding. At a party on deck later in the week for several newly married couples, they were singled out as having been married the shortest time. From deck they all marched into the dining room where for dessert a special cake, with one candle, was brought to their table and sliced with the sword of one of the naval officers present. Speeches followed and it "was all lots of fun."

A typhoon descended, putting Evelyn back in her bunk, very seasick. On the 14th they docked at Kobe, Japan, where they got off and did some sightseeing and shopping. The next day they went to the Oriental Hotel, where she saw celebrity journalist Dorothy Dix and he bought his new bride some "crystals." They sailed at three p.m., with only two days of their voyage remaining.

For August 17 her diary entry reads: "Landed in Shanghai about 6:30 [in the morning]. Came ashore at 9:00. . ."

They immediately hailed a ricksha and rode across the Bund to the Astor House.

At Home in Tientsin

Shanghai, for the next four weeks, became a whirl of welcoming parties for the new Mr. and Mrs. Tucker as well as, for her, an introduction to China. She met many of her new husband's friends—he had been a long-time bachelor and his bride was the object of much interest. She also met "the top brass" of the BAT and was initiated into some of their ways. Despite being a little overwhelmed, she took to the new routine with no apparent difficulty and enjoyed the social events in her honor.

In the meantime foreign newspapers and many private conversations focused on the Japanese, now taking another giant step in their grand imperial plan to take over China and east Asia. Marching still more troops into Manchuria and occupying Mukden, the Japanese declared this huge northern province of China now under their control, renaming it Manchukuo. No one seemed unduly concerned. In what some have called the first chapter of World War II, this started a series of events that eventually affected not only China and her people, but every foreigner—and in particular every American—in the country. My mother and father would be no exception.

Upon their arrival in Shanghai the couple had gone at once to the elegant Astor House, but stayed only one night. With no idea how long they might be in the city, they took a suite at the new apartment-hotel, the Cathay Mansions, in the French Concession. Since the Company usually did not send its married men into the interior of China, he was expecting a new assignment.

On September 15, earlier than expected, he received word of his transfer to Tientsin, in north China, not too far from Manchuria. It was a welcome location because A. P. Tucker—"Tuck"—and his family were there. This was the first cousin from Virginia who had come out to China in 1916 and later had encouraged him to join the BAT.

The couple left Shanghai the next day around noon aboard the Chinese ship *Lu Song*. Two and a half days later, early in the morning, they docked at the small port near Tientsin and caught the train—running five hours late—into the city, arriving around two in the afternoon. Evelyn had been seasick and it was not an auspicious beginning. They checked into the Tientsin Astor House, across the street from the beautiful Victoria Park. Here a suite of rooms would be their home for more than a year.

The next day, a Sunday, Tuck called, inviting the newcomers to dinner with his wife Laura and their small daughter Jean. Afterward they all went to a ballgame. Although the two women had not known each other before and were not the same age, they became lifelong friends, the older doing much to ease the way for the younger.

Once again the new bride enjoyed a round of parties and social events. She made a formal call on the wife of the U.S.

consul-general, a Mrs. Lockhart, and she herself was called on by various ladies of the Tientsin British-American colony. She got to know the other BAT wives as well as other Americans, particularly those connected with the Standard Oil and Texas Oil Companies.

Her diary reveals a social calendar filled with teas and tea dances, dinners, luncheons or "tiffins," bridge parties, cocktail parties and formal dances, including the annual Russian Ball. They also attended barbecues, bowling matches, horse races, poker games, baseball games and countless movies. In turn they entertained that winter at a large cocktail party and at several tiffins and bridge games, along with many smaller dinners to which they invited Laura and Tuck and other couples.

A social highlight of the season was a three-day Chinese wedding; the son of the "No. 1" Chinese at the factory was marrying the daughter of another prominent family in the city. The new Mr. and Mrs. Tucker attended for one afternoon and she was quite the center of attention. The Chinese bride was not due to arrive until the third day but Evelyn met the groom and was shown the vast array of gifts sent by both families—diamonds, jade pieces, pearls, other jewels, bolts of silk for dresses, furs, ceramic dishes, countless beautiful artifacts. She was invited into the matriarch's suite and introduced to her daughters and grandchildren. Here one daughter asked very kindly if she would remove her hat so they could feel her hair, which they greatly admired. Another daughter expressed her deep concern that Mrs. Tucker had been married a year and had not yet presented her husband with a baby. They stayed several hours but left before the evening meal, she, exhausted.

She spent her days writing letters home, visiting with other wives and shopping with another young wife who lived at their hotel. She had her hair "waved," attended a Max Factor Make-up class, went to the dentist twice and got a driver's license so she could drive around on her own in their new Ford, due to arrive soon from the States. She went to a tailor to have a red coat and matching dress made to order and also had several pairs of shoes custom made. And she noted that one afternoon Mr. Chang, the head Chinese at the company, "took Jake and me to look at furs. . ." A day or so later she "selected my fur coat."

There were times when Evelyn was homesick. She and Jake made a point of having Thanksgiving dinner with Laura and Tuck—it seemed a touch of home. They often had meals together and shared news, passing on the latest about relatives and friends in Virginia. Her diary for December 25th reads, "Christmas Day and I'm 10,000 miles away from home. . ."

Letters did, however, make things easier. Mail crossing the Pacific Ocean, both eastward and westward, traveled by ship, following no schedule and adhering to no timetable. The arrival in La Crosse of a letter from China was always met with much rejoicing; it would be dutifully sent or read to one relative after another. And the arrival in China of a letter from home was cause for celebration. Her mother and sister wrote regularly, as did his mother, and she also corresponded with several friends and other relatives. Only a few of these survived the years.

One long letter from her mother was dated Saturday night, October 31, 1931. The following are excerpts:

> *My precious baby child:*
> *I spent today at Woodlands. . . .I found Miss Nelly up and fully dressed. . . .She asked about you right away, and said she feels as proud of your <u>conquest</u> as we do. She also said, "Mrs.*

Harrison, there are not many girls whose lives have fallen in such pleasant places as Evelyn's."

There were also some words about marriage and life in general for this daughter who was so very far away:

The comradeship and close communion of a marriage where there is complete love and congeniality, is a partnership, a consolidation of forces, a source of purposeful incentive towards a shared goal, and with a jewel of a husband such as you have, can mean but one thing—a lovely journey through life.

Her mother mentions three neighborhood children who were eager to get the Chinese stamps from her letters and includes bits of news she knew would be of interest. There are requests for pictures "of you and Jake" and a description of "your newest evening dress," along with some other comments:

...Ma [her grandmother Bowen] *has just come in with a big plate of peanut candy, and she said, "I wish Evelyn had some of it." She has a cry over every letter from you, but she says it's from joy over your happiness. . . Charlie* [Agnes' husband] *said last night, "Evelyn married the right man because she isn't the kind that could work, she isn't built that way."*

Several remarks reveal how much her daughter's letters meant to this mother: "I had been [home] only a few minutes, when Marjorie came in with a letter from <u>you</u>, which meant the end of a perfect day for me." And "I enjoy your letters so much, and nothing is too insignificant to relate. . . ."

The new Mr. and Mrs. Tucker ushered in 1932 at a masquerade ball and in the new year kept up the accustomed social pace. During that summer, though, they accepted Laura's invitation to move into their house while she and Jean spent the summer at Peitaho on the beach—Tuck would stay at a hotel during the week. Evelyn and Jake visited once or twice but Evelyn didn't much care for Peitaho. It boasted a fine beach but only some small cottages on the ocean. There were "no movies, no cars, etc....It's just a small village by the sea with donkeys to ride on and a train a day."

In the meantime my parents continued to enjoy the social scene in Tientsin and that fall moved into a house directly across the street from Laura and Tuck. "I'll have a living room," she wrote home, "dining room, kitchen and there are three bedrooms but I'm only using two and two baths. . . "

In October they took a long weekend trip with friends to Peking. Here they rented a car, visited some BAT officials, and drove out to see the "Temple of Heaven" and the Summer Palace. She also did some shopping, buying several pieces of needlework including a chrysanthemum brocade hanging of exquisite handiwork that the merchant claimed was over 150 years old.

In the middle of January Evelyn received a letter from her sister telling her of their mother's long and severe illness. A few days later the cable came reporting her mother's death at the age of fifty-eight from complications following gallbladder surgery. On the 17th she wrote in her diary: "The Cable came this p.m. I don't feel that I'll ever care to write in here again, so this ends My Diary." She never even opened it again.

My mother's grief, mixed with guilt for being so far away from home, was deep and long-lasting. Of concern, too, was the financial condition of her family, suffering greatly during the nationwide Depression of those years. There are hints that she herself battled with illness, perhaps the depression that was to recur at various times throughout her life.

But life went on, even in China, and the months passed.

I was born in August of 1934. And given her mother's name, Leta May.

China Born

China born.

Born outside of the United States. Away from "home." Stranger in a foreign land. Wherever I was, that fact would forever define me. Always I would feel "different" from those around me.

China born.

Softly, with barely a warning whisper, China slipped into my life and left her indelible mark—sharp and deep, delicate and beautiful, squalid and sinister. As quiet as my amah's padded footsteps beside my baby bed, as persistent as the street hawker's early morning chants beneath my open window, as pervasive as the smells of garlic and sweet sandalwood drifting in the air around me, China laid claim to a part of me and never quite relinquished her hold.

Always in the background there was China. I came to marvel at the beauty of her ancient culture and to ache with the misery of her people. Like the Yang and Yin of Chinese philosophy, China was irrevocably entwined with my American self, sometimes dominant, sometimes hidden, almost, for a time forgotten—but always present. Although I chose sometimes not to see it and often could not explain it, China shadowed my life, influenced my character, filtered into my mind—and settled into a corner of my heart.

Woven into my days from the beginning were things Chinese: bowls of rice and pots of tea; exquisite silks and lovely linens; delicate porcelain and soft, thick green rugs; the blue satin slippers with their red flowers my amah made for me; the carved wooden junk that sat on our living room mantle. A favorite plaything was our mah jong set—the smooth ivory tiles were cool to my touch and made a soft, muffled, clicking sound as I moved them around. My first words were Chinese—I talked to our servants before I spoke English with my parents. I basked in the smiles that a small child— even a foreign one—always brought to the faces of older Chinese. I loved ricksha rides with Amah, Chinese chow for tiffin and my Chinese name, "Mei Li."

China born. And yet, although immersed in China and Chinese life, I was so American. My birth certificate was a form entitled *Report of Birth: Child Born Abroad of an American Father.* Signed by the United States Consul-General, it listed pertinent data about my parents and the fact that I was born at five o'clock on the morning of Tuesday, August 14, 1934 at the German-American Hospital in Tientsin. One copy was placed "under File No. 131 in the archives of this office," one went to the State Department in Washington, D.C., and one was given to my parents. Eventually their copy would come to me, with instructions to guard it carefully; it was my proof of American citizenship.

From an early age I was aware that I was an American. Though ignorant of details, I understood that this was very important, something I must never forget. It distinguished me from others around me and put me in a special category. Above all it assured my safety in times of danger, giving me immunity from harm. Even the word "America" seemed magic; it meant happy people and a beautiful land far across the sea. In a letter home when I was barely three, my mother wrote of me: "She talks a lot about going to America—I think she is expecting to see wonderful things."

I was in China, of course, because my parents were in China. My father, thirty-eight years old when I was born, had been for over ten years with the British American Tobacco Company. Cigarettes, cigars and tobacco were not then considered the evils they were later to become, and the tobacco market in China was vast and lucrative. He enjoyed the work and the way of life it made possible and found China, whose strife with Japan was escalating all around him, a fascinating country.

My mother, too, was enchanted by China, especially the northern city of Tientsin where they were assigned. She liked the life style it allowed Westerners to lead, appreciated her role as a company wife and enjoyed traveling in society "first-class." When I was born she was twenty-nine and easily adapted to some of the customs of both British and American friends in this foreign city. Upon my birth she immediately hired a Chinese amah, or nanny, who had almost complete care of me.

I weighed seven and a half pounds at birth, had big fat cheeks, enormous blue eyes—and no hair. Since my mother cut off the one small curl at the back of my neck for my baby book, for the next two years and more my head was covered only with a fine blond fuzz. Meanwhile my amah carefully saved my every trimmed fingernail and toenail to keep "the evil one" from finding them and casting over me an evil spell.

I lived in Tientsin only about nine months. In the spring of 1935 my father was eligible for home leave, and in April we sailed for America on the SS *President Coolidge*. Our trip took us to Japan, Hawaii, California and across the States to southern Virginia.

In Virginia we visited with family over the next four months. Photographs show a dozen or so aunts and uncles and cousins posing with me, along with one young colored girl named Helen who helped look after me. I became very fond of her and clung to her amid the confusion of lots of relatives. Those snapshots were carefully placed in a scrapbook, helping me to identify the many members of my family.

In late August we sailed from San Francisco on the *President Cleveland*, bound for Honolulu, Yokohama and Shanghai. On the day we docked at the Shanghai Bund an American newspaper welcomed the liner and its passengers, noting that they were arriving "in the coldest weather since last spring. . ."

On its front page the newspaper ran a photograph of me in my stroller, with the caption: "First prize among the babies went to blue-eyed, golden haired little Miss Tucker. . . for all the world the most serious and curious passenger on board. Wrapped in her warm pink sweater, she was entirely oblivious to the cold. . . .And as for her curiosity, everyone was subjected to her scrutinizing stare."

We stayed for several months in Shanghai. My father was then assigned, with his family, to Hankow, some seven hundred miles up the Yangtze. We would not be returning to Tientsin. Nor would I ever again see the city of my birth.

In Hankow as they did in Shanghai and, indeed, throughout the Orient, the British and the Americans enjoyed a most pleasurable life style. It was a way of life that was to disappear completely over the next ten years.

It was a way of life, too, that would be directly affected by the actions and decisions of governments, particularly those of China and Japan. I was three years old when I faced the first of these major disruptions in my life.

Bloody Saturday

Carefully, so as not to be noticed, I picked up one more candle and pushed it gently into the top of my birthday cake. It stood easily next to the other three my mother had just arranged and four did look so much better. Besides, the Chinese counted one's arrival in the world as the first birthday—Amah and Cook, who had baked me this special cake, called me four years old. But whenever my parents and their friends asked my age, I held up only three fingers.

It was Saturday, August 14, 1937—my birthday. The day would mark my first conscious memory. And it would go down in Shanghai history as "Bloody Saturday."

We had only been in Shanghai two months. For the past year we had been living in Hankow, up the Yangtze River about seven hundred fifty miles, where my father was manager of the BAT factory. Besides growing tobacco the Chinese working under him raised pigs, chickens and geese and grew both vegetables and flowers. Although I don't remember it, my mother and I often left our apartment on those lovely spring days to ride out to the factory compound to spend a few hours "in the country."

Our days in Hankow, however, were not to last. One morning in June my father received a wire from company headquarters ordering him to come immediately to Shanghai. He was to go by plane and since it was his first airplane flight he was nervous. The next day he returned with the news that we were to leave Hankow as soon as possible. Two days later we boarded a riverboat for Shanghai. The company, concerned for the safety of their employees' families, was ordering those in certain areas to leave at once due to the worsening situation with the Japanese in northeastern and central China. My father, still assigned to the Hankow factory, would return for weeks at the time, but we would live in Shanghai.

Talk of war was not new to Americans and Britishers living in China—there was always talk of war. But now the Japanese, having successfully taken over Manchuria, were threatening the armies of Chiang Kai Shek in north China and pushing farther and farther inland and to the south. Since the last Sino-Japanese conflict in 1932, relations between the two countries had grown increasingly tense and had now again reached the brink of war. Other nations, assuming that only China and Japan would be involved, left the two long-time enemies to fight it out among themselves.

Foreigners in Shanghai noticed the increasing tension. After a series of incidents between Chinese and Japanese in and around the city, they expected hostilities of some sort to break out somewhere at any time. Conspicuous in the Whangpoo River were the Japanese ship *Idzumo*, a British gunboat, the *H.M.S. Falmouth*, and a U.S. naval vessel, the *U.S.S. Augusta*, flagship of the U.S. Asiatic fleet, back from Hankow, where my parents had been among those Americans invited to a reception on board. The presence of U.S. Marines on the river always provided a security blanket much appreciated by all Americans. Confident that neither Japanese or Chinese would dare touch the French Concession or the International Settlement, nor any British or American citizen, people were not overly worried.

In Shanghai we were living at the apartment of company friends away on home-leave. Cavendish Court—quiet and serene within its tree-lined compound—was far out Avenue Petain, in the western part of the French Concession. My parents had several good friends living nearby who telephoned or visited frequently. With my father back in Hankow, my mother, six months pregnant, confessed only to feeling "a bit nervous."

On the morning of Friday, August 13, my mother, with our chauffeur, Mo Ling, set out for Wingon's Department Store down on Nanking Road to do some shopping. She was looking for a birthday present for me—a doll carriage. She found, she later wrote her sister, "a lovely English pram."

As they neared the Bund she noticed more activity than usual on the streets, with swarms of people everywhere, and from the Chinese settlement in the distance she could hear sporadic machine gun fire. Inside the store word was spreading that after months of tension, Chinese and Japanese troops had begun bombarding each other in the Chapei section of the city. The sound of artillery was becoming louder and more constant. Having found my present, she decided to cut short her shopping trip and hurried back to the car, telling Mo Ling to drive straight home.

Throngs of people choked the Bund and Avenue Edward VII. Cars could only inch along, penned in on all sides. Foreigners as well as Chinese peasants, carrying all they owned, were fleeing across the Garden Bridge out of Japanese Hongkew, trying to reach the safe areas of the International Settlement and the French Concession.

As one newspaper reported it: "...Panic seized many thousands of Chinese in the vicinity, and they fled in hordes for the Settlement area south of the Creek...Hundreds of civilians who had waited till the last moment before evacuating to the safer precincts of the Settlement, hurriedly packed their belongings and ran most of the way, as hardly any vehicles were available..."

Mo Ling got my mother safely back to the apartment where, she wrote her sister, she "sat all afternoon listening to bombs and machine guns" in the eastern and northern sections of the city. She felt relatively safe in Frenchtown. But the radio began to report the escalation of fighting and she grew uneasy. Around nine that night she tried to telephone my father in Hankow, only to be told that it was "impossible." So she went to bed, getting little sleep.

The next morning, the 14th, the city awoke to a state bordering on war. Machine gun fire was louder, more intense and more widespread. The Japanese continued to shell Chinese Chapei. Many firms suspended business. Chinese banks closed. Telephone calls were twenty minutes and more in getting connected. Men in the Shanghai Volunteer Corps, the foreign defense group, were being mobilized. Old ships had been scuttled overnight and were being used to block the Whangpoo River above the city. Barbed wire "entanglements" had hurriedly gone up at many street intersections. Sand bag barricades were being installed at specified points. Along the Bund the entrances to many buildings were hidden behind huge mounds of sand bags.

Japanese soldiers had now taken over the Eight Character Bridge leading into Chinese Chapei. They also manned pill boxes hastily put up in Hongkew. Joining the *Idzumo* in the harbor were four Japanese cruisers and seven destroyers. To "insure safety" they landed 3,500 additional Japanese marines in Hongkew. Japanese "aeroplanes" from points north had already taken to the skies across China, many headed for Shanghai. And down in the China Sea, just beyond the Yangtze, sat the Japanese Third Fleet.

The Chinese, limited by complicated treaty stipulations, faced overwhelming difficulties in trying to defend themselves in this international city. Just outside the International Settlement itself, however, were stationed two divisions of Chinese troops—an estimated 30,000 men. From rural areas in the country's interior her airplane pilots, poorly trained though they were, set out for Shanghai and the Whangpoo. They had orders to bomb the *Idzumo* and other Japanese ships as well as targets in Hongkew.

In the International Settlement, overrun with throngs of Chinese peasants, and in the French Concession, quickly filling with outsiders, officials were addressing the emergency, implementing the mechanics of caring for refugees and providing protection for foreigners. The initial stages for controlling the distribution of food and fuel were being put in place. Authorities were also reviewing detailed procedures for the evacuation of residents. Officials, as well as residents, remembering their lax response and subsequent danger in 1932, were now seriously worried about the current conflict.

Meanwhile my father and two other company men, faced with a growing Japanese presence in the interior, were making plans to leave Hankow. Despite the threat of a typhoon, early on Saturday they flew to Shanghai, landing at an airfield miles out in the country. With no transportation available, they walked several miles up a railroad track to the outskirts of the city. Around 10:30 he telephoned my mother, and a few minutes later, rumpled, muddy and tired, he walked in our front door. She took one look at him and burst into tears. His was the last plane out of Hankow, and later that day the Japanese destroyed the airfield where they had landed.

Since it was my birthday, and we knew no children nearby, a few of my mother's friends had been invited to drop in around four o'clock for tea and birthday cake. My father called in a few more friends to help celebrate his escape from Hankow, serving something a little stronger than tea. There was even a toast to "Tuckey," as my father called me—a nickname he gave me after I once mispronounced my last name.

I stayed busy with my gifts while the grown-ups stood on our sixth floor veranda and watched the fringes of war miles away in the eastern and northern parts of the city. Every few minutes they had to stop talking while a Chinese plane flew very low over us. I got up once and went over by my mother to look. I didn't like the roar of the planes and went back inside to my ice cream and my cake, still bearing its four candles.

It was while we were having tea that four Chinese planes flew down the Whangpoo, intending to bomb Japanese ships. Instead, missing their targets, two veered toward the Bund and dropped two bombs on that crowded thoroughfare, one at the entrance to the Cathay Hotel and the other on the roof of the Palace Hotel. Hundreds of people, Chinese and foreign, all innocent civilians, were killed or severely injured. The resulting panic and devastation—the streets were said to run with blood—were terrible. One newspaper noted that there were not nearly enough ambulances to carry the injured to the various hospitals, nor enough doctors to treat all who had been hit. Many spoke of the audacity of the planes in coming even close to the foreign settlements. More destruction, however, was yet to come.

Shortly afterward occurred the second catastrophe of the day. A lone Chinese plane, damaged by Japanese fire and appearing lost, dropped two bombs in the middle of a main intersection at Avenue Edward VII—a busy street normally and now swarming with thousands of homeless refugees.

"The slaughter," wrote an American reporter, "was appalling." According to one report there were "well over 1,500" casualties, including foreigners and Chinese; others placed the number at 2,000. Thirty-seven truckloads of dead were later removed from the scene.

At first people assumed that the Japanese were responsible for the bombing. They could not believe that the Chinese had dropped bombs on their own people, in their own city. And they were shocked that either the Japanese or the Chinese could even think of endangering the invulnerable International Settlement. The truth appeared to be that Chinese planes, missing their targets, had dropped the bombs "by accident." Even with that explanation and an official apology from Generalissimo and Madame Chiang Kai Shek, Westerners remained stunned and distraught. The unthinkable had happened: British and American subjects had been killed within Shanghai's foreign concessions and those concessions themselves had been attacked. Newspapers called it "Bloody Saturday," a day that "no Shanghailander would ever forget."

A state of undeclared war between China and Japan now existed in Hongkew and Chapei and on the Whangpoo and Yangtze Rivers. The bombing and shelling continued throughout the night. Machine gun fire and other artillery fire could be heard everywhere.

The International Settlement and the French Concession were like a walled city within a city—and not all that safe. All foreigners, some still trying to account for missing individuals caught in the bombings, were alarmed. Stories spread of residents dodging stray bullets in their own living rooms. The entire city was in turmoil.

By Sunday night martial law was declared and in the settlements no unauthorized person was allowed on the streets after 10 p.m. In the French Concession authorities placed anti-aircraft guns on top of their tall buildings—several were on the Picardie Apartment House across the street from us. Both Japanese and Chinese authorities were warned that if they even flew their war planes over Frenchtown they would be "dealt with accordingly."

Government officials, deeply concerned, were taking appropriate steps to protect their nationals. On Sunday the British Consul-General ordered all British women and children to evacuate to Hong Kong. On Monday morning the American Consul-General and the Admiral of the U.S. Asiatic Fleet met and issued orders for the evacuation of all American women and children to Manila, in the Philippines, then a U.S. Territory. The earliest anyone could leave would be Tuesday.

My father immediately went down to arrange passage for my mother and me, along with three BAT wives, close friends, whose husbands were not in Shanghai. He got space for us on the *President Jefferson* leaving the next day—the first of the refugee ships out. Amah helped my mother pack two small suitcases and the next morning at nine we drove down to the Dollar Line pier on the Bund.

I could feel the heavy tension surrounding my father and mother. She expressed her feelings later in a letter to her family. ". . .No one knows," she wrote, "how I dreaded to tell Jake good-bye & start out on that trip. . .It was awful."

Refugees

$\mathcal{B}$y nine o'clock on Tuesday morning, with Mo Ling at the wheel, my father, my mother and I had made our way past barricaded streets and blocks of destruction to the Bund and the Customs Jetty. Although it was August the typhoon of the past few days still lingered and it was cool; I wore my blue sweater. The Whangpoo looked muddier than ever and a strong wind ruffled the water.

Ahead of us, at the Dollar Line pier, we could see the tender that my mother and I would board to go down river to the *President Jefferson*. Stretched across her funnel was a huge American flag, on this gray day its bright red, white and blue a reassuring sight. On her deck and along the pier moved dozens of United States Marines. At the gangplank were assembled a portion of the American women and children obeying their government's order to evacuate Shanghai.

A good number of those gathered on the pier knew each other; there were quiet greetings and friendly talking. Many of the women were pregnant, many carried babies and some also held another small child by the hand. All were trying to be brave and cheerful. Their husbands would remain behind, of course, and the wives knew that as long as the war continued it might be months before they saw them again or could return to their homes. Very little could be packed in the two small suitcases they were authorized to take on board—but it would have to do.

We were soon joined by the three other company wives traveling with us. My father took us as close to the gangplank as he could, and after a few minutes said goodby and left us. He would wait with others along the pier to see us off. A Marine took our suitcases and led us up the gangplank. On board, another led us into the large main cabin, telling us to "take cover."

The luxury liner *President Jefferson* had long been scheduled to stop at Shanghai on this day to pick up passengers booked for a routine voyage to Seattle. With the crisis in Shanghai, the Consul-General had requested that the *Jefferson* make room for American evacuees and detour to Manila. This was the first of the U.S. ships to be so activated. Two more liners, the *President Hoover* and the *President McKinley* would follow in the next few days, carrying more Americans safely out of China.

It had been expected that the *Jefferson* would come up the Whangpoo to the Shanghai pier. The continued bombing, however, apparently posed too many difficulties. Nor did she come up the Yangtze to Woosung at the mouth of the Whangpoo. Instead she was anchored out in the China Sea, miles away, waiting for the tender with its four hundred women and children to come out to her. Japanese destroyers and other vessels were moving up both rivers, and nine Japanese battleships surrounded the liner out in the sea. Chinese airplanes were continuing their bombing raids.

Their main targets: the Japanese ships.

Further down the Whangpoo pier from the American tender were gathered over a thousand British subjects ordered to Hong Kong. They also were to be evacuated this morning. Their ship, the British *Rajputana*, was to come up the Yangtze to Woosung, where their women and children would board. The British tenders were flying "the white Ensign." All of the refugee tenders, both British and American, with their large flags highly visible, could be easily and immediately recognized.

Concerned about the logistics of safely moving so many women and children, British and American authorities had informed both Chinese and Japanese officials of their respective evacuation plans. Both were asked to refrain from any bombing or other military maneuvers while the passengers were boarding and during their trip down river to meet their ships. Both agreed to cooperate and honor the request.

Right on schedule the American tender prepared to leave. The Marines stayed on board, most of them visible on deck. Into the main cabin as well as below deck were crowded 410 women and children.

Just as the tender pulled away from the pier, three Chinese planes appeared in the sky over Pootung, to the east, headed for the *Idzumo*. As the Chinese dropped their bombs Japanese ships in the harbor at once opened fire with their anti-aircraft guns. Neither side made any pretense of keeping a truce. British and American ships in the harbor could do nothing.

Horrified, passengers on the tender were frightened and enraged at this betrayal of trust. They knew that if a bomb or shell hit them—trapped, with no way to escape—most would surely perish.

On shore my father and the other husbands watched as the

tender left the pier. Seeing the Chinese planes approaching the Whangpoo, they were alarmed—and angry. The most basic of humanitarian gestures allowed for the protection of women and children. Stunned at this breach of faith on the part of so-called "friends," with some voicing dismay at their own government for allowing this to happen, all they could do was stand and watch.

For a few minutes it looked like the little tender, carrying double its capacity, fighting choppy waves and a strong wind and trying to avoid bombs and shells, would capsize before their very eyes. Witnesses wondered if it would ever make it down to the main ship. But somehow it managed to slowly push on down the river, out of their sight and past Japanese destroyers coming up into the harbor.

On board, no passengers were on deck; all had taken cover in the cabins. All available seats were taken. Some stood. Others sat on the floor. One corner near us was draped with sheets; on a cot behind it a woman was in labor. With so many crowded together in such a small space it was hot and uncomfortable.

My mother was sitting on a bench, while I stood right beside her. I had tried to sit on the bench, too, but I kept sliding off. With one hand I gripped a small red and yellow change purse—a birthday present; inside was the Chinese dollar Daddy had given me. With my other hand I clutched my mother's dark blue skirt.

It took hours for our tender to get down the river. At Woosung at the mouth of the Whangpoo, we passed the *Rajputana* coming in, while we struggled on toward the *Jefferson* still eight miles out. Leaving the Whangpoo we headed into the Yangtze and the open sea. Not meant for anything other than river travel and carrying twice its normal load, the tender now contended with a worsening wind, a strong tide and a heavy sea—all were making her progress difficult and threatening the vessel itself.

Most of the women tried to stay calm and to reassure each other, as well as the children. But the floor kept rising and then falling, and then rolling from side to side. Anything not fastened or held down rolled or bounced across the floor. The ship heaved so badly that passengers couldn't stand up and were being thrown about the large cabin. All were in danger of being injured. A few people were seasick, a few fainted. Many of the children began screaming and crying.

My mother and I stayed very still in the midst of the crowd of people, surrounded by confusion and noise. I didn't cry. But it must have been about this time that I whispered to her, "Mommy, I don't like this. I want to go home."

The tender finally reached the *Jefferson* through seas so heavy that many watching from that ship as well as some on the tender thought we would not make it. The larger ship was swinging around in the strong current and could not lie still, so that the tender had great difficulty even getting near it.

The *Jefferson's* captain at first refused to even attempt to transfer any passengers. But we couldn't go back. The tide was too strong for the overloaded tender to try to get back to the river to wait for the liner to come in. It was too late for other plans. They had to take us on board.

Though there was no panic, the passengers were reaching the end of their endurance. As my mother later wrote, ". . .when we passed between the Jap. war ships [we] held [our] breath. Then when we got into rough water and the boat nearly capsized, well it almost proved too much for us."

With no other option, the captain finally decided to risk the transfer. The tender managed to maneuver into the lee side of the liner and a gangplank was laid between her deck and a port on the liner. Marines formed a tight row on each side of the gangplank. As the passengers came out on deck each was almost bodily moved from one Marine to the next, up the line to a waiting crew member at the larger ship. Everything had to be done quickly, before the ship moved too much. It stayed still just long enough.

When my mother and I stepped out on deck the wind was blowing hard and the gangplank swayed badly. One Marine, a large blond man, reached to pick me up and then dropped me—I could see the ocean below me through the cracks of the gangplank. He quickly snatched me up and passed me on to another and another and then inside the ship.

Finally we were all safely on board the *Jefferson*. To many it seemed a miracle. Most could only be grateful that the mission was accomplished and no one was hurt—at least physically. The Marines and the liner's crew deserved much credit. The officers of the *Jefferson* were commended for their excellent seamanship and the Marines especially praised for their handling of the women and children on the tender, averting what would surely have been a terrible disaster.

On the liner the scheduled passengers graciously moved over to make room for four hundred bewildered fellow Americans. The crew did all they could to help, and accommodations of some sort were found for everyone. Crowded though it was, the ship turned toward the Philippines.

In the coming months there were those who seriously questioned the actions of the American authorities in allowing such a situation as we experienced to develop. Why, they asked, could not the *Jefferson*, like the *Rajputana*, at least have come up to the Whangpoo to receive the refugees? If this were not possible, why was not one of the American ships in the harbor used as a visible escort for the tender in the middle of the Japanese fleet? Why, indeed, were the lives of these American women and children put at such risk? Satisfactory answers were never given. It was later revealed that the *Jefferson* did receive an order to go and meet the tender at the river—after we were all on board.

We reached Manila on August 20th, the fourth day out, late in the afternoon. Boarding the ship before we could dock were officials of the Quarantine Office, concerned that the refugees might be bringing the seeds of epidemics with them. We were all immediately given shots for typhoid, cholera and dysentery.

At seven that evening we pulled into Manila's Pier 7. While we, as a part of the BAT "family" were advised to stay on board over night until our permanent accommodations were ready, many passengers immediately disembarked. Within the hour Manila experienced a devastating earthquake—the worst in years—and everyone on land was terrified. For those still on the ship the experience, though less severe, was still frightening, but no one was hurt and there was little damage to the ship.

Despite the earthquake the Philippines for six months proved a safe haven. The BAT families were taken from Manila to a large sugar plantation whose American owner had generously offered us its elaborate "country club" facilities. We all enjoyed the pool, the excellent food and the luxurious rooms.

In October my father, worried about my mother, flew down from Shanghai. Within a few days he moved us to a resort hotel in Baguio to be closer to doctors and a hospital. My brother Bill was born there on November 9.

I was delighted to have a brother. All the little boys I knew had dozens of small metal cars that they spent hours rolling across the floor and tables. I had requested a car and been told that little girls did not play with cars. I was sure that a brother would somehow share his when he grew older.

Daddy soon left to return to China. After being held up in Hong Kong for days until the war situation grew quieter, he and over seven hundred returning refugees arrived back in Shanghai. Although still officially assigned to Hankow, now under Japanese control, he was given temporary duties in company factories in Shanghai.

For weeks in December and January my mother tried to book passage to Shanghai but was told that due to the Chinese-Japanese war there were no ships going to the city. Despondent and lonely, she even considered going instead to the States. All this time my brother was staying in the nursery at the Catholic hospital where he was born. Mama and I spent hours there every day, she deeply grateful to the kind nuns who were so helpful.

At last we sailed for Hong Kong, where my father met us. After a few days there we continued on to Shanghai, arriving on February 1, among still more refugees now making their way back home.

Home to Shanghai

Aboard the Italian liner *Conte Rossa* on a cold day in February, 1938 we sailed up the Yangtze to Woosung, on up the Whangpoo and back to Shanghai. Instead of passing under the guns of the Japanese fleet as we had six months earlier, now we passed only a few Chinese junks. As my mother wrote in a letter home, along each side of the river was widespread devastation; no one was to be seen and over everything hung a death-like stillness. It was a different China, a different Shanghai, that greeted us on our return.

From now on my China home would be Shanghai. The first four years of my life—from 1934 to 1938—had been spent in such places as Tientsin, Hankow and Kuling, a mountain resort. During those years we were constantly on the move, not only from city to city but from apartment to friend's house to another apartment. We spent five months on home leave in the States in 1935 and then were evacuated to the Philippines in 1937. From 1938 on, Shanghai was home and the place I knew best.

We were back in Shanghai only because the war had moved elsewhere. The Japanese, wherever they had presented themselves, were without question the victors. The past six months had brought the occupation of Chinese Shanghai, the attack on the British ship *Petrel,* the sinking of the U.S. gunboat *Panay,* and the occupation and rape of Nanking—the latter a horror ignored by many. Thumbing their noses at Westerners in Shanghai, the Japanese military had roared through the city like a typhoon, depositing several thousand additional marines in Hongkew—who remained there "to keep order"—and establishing their control in the city in spite of the remaining British and Americans.

The city had suffered in many ways. Thousands of Chinese civilians had been killed or displaced. Major industries and small storekeepers as well were directly affected. My mother and her friends deplored the loss of dozens of quaint little shops carrying beautiful linens, curios and silks, where they often had shopped; now they were either a pile of rubble or boarded up. My father's factory had not been bombed but still showed much damage. Everything had been looted, machinery destroyed and some 12,000 window panes broken. Inside the compound returning workers found dead soldiers, severed heads and other evidence of fighting. Now the war had moved up the Yangtze and into China's interior. Once again Shanghai had survived and set about returning to life as usual.

Even to a child's eyes Shanghai was an extraordinary place. I gradually became aware of all kinds of different people around me. Most of my parents' friends were American or British and so were most of my playmates, but I sometimes played with children who were Russian, French, German or Swiss.

The city was home to some thirty different nationalities, people who differed greatly in dress, language, background, behavior and physical appearance. Some that I saw on a routine basis I learned to identify. The small exclusive dress shops and boutiques where my mother sometimes shopped, occasionally letting me tag along, were often run by French women, sophisticated and elegant in their stylish dresses, bright red nail polish and glittering jewelry. They spoke in rapid high-pitched voices and were not fond of children— even very quiet little girls.

The city was also home to many "White Russians." Once politically aligned with their tsar and the royal family, twenty years earlier they had escaped the 1917 Revolution in their country and fled to Shanghai. Some of them, along with many Jewish families, owned a variety of restaurants and shops on Avenue Joffre near our apartment. In one dark, crowded family establishment a large woman with black hair always looked so sad as she counted out yarn for my mother, selected a blouse for me or measured my fist to determine the correct size for my new socks. Sometimes, though, she smiled, and once she gave me a present—a pretty blue hair ribbon.

Easy to recognize in their high pink or white turbans were the tall, powerful Sikhs who served as police, keeping order in the French Concession. They directed traffic at street intersections, blowing their whistles and swinging and pointing their long arms at cars. Near my father's office in Hongkew, Japanese soldiers patrolled the streets—in full uniform, with guns and bayonets.

Chinese were, of course, the most numerous of the masses of people who lived in Shanghai. Speaking many dialects and varying in physical appearance, they came from all over the country to settle in this city of possibilities. Theirs was a class society and the divisions were easy to distinguish. I sometimes glimpsed the very wealthy riding through the city in their long black foreign-made limousines, the women in silk brocade Chinese-style dresses and furs, the men wearing their affluence along with their European-style suits. When I visited my father's factory the top Chinese staff greeted me in English; Chinese workers of a lower class operated the cigarette machines. Of higher status were our amah and house servants, and those of our friends. Anyone speaking English was considered a cut above those who could not.

At the bottom of the system were the beggars and coolies. Coolies pulled rickshas with passengers, carried produce and other goods on bamboo poles balanced across their shoulders, performed all kinds of heavy manual labor and hauled away the daily "honey carts" of human refuse from the poor parts of the city. The filthy beggars lining the streets, accosting foreigners for money, showed varying stages of need and physical deformities, from blindness to severed limbs to starvation. I learned early that the material wealth of this world is not distributed equally to all. In Shanghai it was obvious everywhere I looked.

Shanghai's government was also unusual. Although a part of China, the city was not governed by the Chinese, but by major foreign powers under a policy known as *extraterritoriality*. Years earlier, nations beginning to trade with China had simply divided up the new seaport and established their own spheres of influence. Each nation had its own regulations, laws and court systems, its own industrial, commercial and residential areas. As a result no foreign country or its citizens would ever be subject to any Chinese law or authority. Great Britain, France and the United States were the main treaty powers operating under this system of *"extr'ality."* Later other nations, particularly Japan, also claimed rights.

The British and American Concessions eventually combined into the International Settlement, encompassing the Bund and the financial world, export-import companies, commercial and trading firms, factories, hotels, theaters, night clubs and some residences. The French Concession, toward the south and west, was characterized by wide tree-lined boulevards, large houses and villas, private walled-in estates, opulent art deco apartment buildings, smaller homes and countless little stores, shops, restaurants and sidewalk cafes. Here in "Frenchtown," where we always lived, were the homes of most of Shanghai's French and many Americans and British, as well as wealthy Chinese.

Shanghai, with this huge conglomerate of people, during the late 1930s seethed with political unrest, class struggle and a growing dislike of foreigners. Neither my family nor I could escape the warfare that marked these years. Nor could we, as Americans, avoid the longtime hatred that caused some Chinese to refer to us as "foreign devils."

My small life and the world that centered around me were removed as much as possible from the reality of those Shanghai days. Upon our return to the city we moved into the house of company friends on leave in the States. Complete with servants, the house was enclosed in its own compound on Rue de Lastre, with limited access from the street. It was a lovely home and my parents were pleased to be invited to stay there while we waited for an apartment.

Every day I played in the garden with its big stretch of shady grass, swings and beautiful flowers. My new friend Betsy, whose father was also in the BAT, often came to visit. We would have tea parties with our dolls out on the lawn and then my mother or the amah would bring us the makings of a real tea party served under a shade tree on the lawn.

Near my birthday a large package arrived from America with a present for me from my Aunt Nancy. I was thrilled with her gift of a "real" American dress of bright pink, yellow and blue flowered cotton with a full skirt. I wore it along with my Chinese straw hat for my mother to take a photograph to send her.

These were relatively quiet days, but a vivid memory remains of our stay on Rue de Lastre. One night we all were awakened by a loud commotion among the servants, with the watchdog frantically barking. I could hear my father yelling to the head boy and on the stairs some sort of scuffle was taking place. Despite the high wall that surrounded the house and yard, and the fact that several servants, including a night watchman, lived on the grounds, a burglar had gotten inside the compound, broken the panes of the French doors leading from the porch into the living room, and was inside the dining room before anyone was aroused. The intruder, a Chinese, was cornered on the stairs and soon handed over to the local police.

My parents were greatly concerned, suspecting that the break-in was somehow instigated, or at least condoned, by some of the servants. The owners of the house were due back soon from leave and my father had already made plans to move. This time it would be into our own apartment. We had been on the waiting list at the Grosvenor House for some time and now were notified that we could have access. Within days we had left the house on Rue de Lastre.

As protected as I was in my little cocoon, I could not help but see, though at first I little understood, what surrounded me beyond the walls of home. Out in the city itself hunger, filth, crime, confusion, anxiety and fear were everywhere.

Despite its dark side, it was a privileged life style. We were living in the glory days of a cosmopolitan society characterized by varying degrees of wealth and class—residents of an international city dominated by the pursuit of money, adventure and pleasure. Americans and British held a unique position in this society that was, by 1940, vanishing.

For me, at that time, Shanghai was my home. From the time we moved into 303 Grosvenor House I felt at home—and safe.

The Grosvenor House

The Grosvenor House was very big, very British, very 1930s posh—and very safe. The compound with its sixteen story triple-tiered brick apartment building, large enclosed garden and surrounding lower apartment sections, occupied a city block in the French Concession at 219 Rue Cardinal Mercier. Completed only a few years earlier, people considered it one of Shanghai's largest and most elegant art deco apartment compounds.

Our apartment, though numbered 303, was on the fourth floor, following the British custom of not numbering the entrance floor, in the middle section of the main building. We quickly got settled. My parents, delighted with the apartment, began buying furniture. Our new amah arrived the same day we did and took charge of Bill and me. My father, unable to return to Japanese-occupied Hankow, was now assigned to Shanghai, first to the BAT factory in Pootung and later to the Thorburn Roads factory in Hongkew, assuring his continued presence with us.

Our apartment had large, high-ceilinged rooms: a living room, dining room, enclosed veranda, two bedrooms, each with a bath, a kitchen and the servants' quarters. The décor differed for each flat; in ours the walls were painted a soft cream color, the woodwork stained a deep walnut and across the ceilings of each room stretched huge exposed walnut beams. Casement windows with no screens filled one side of each room. The kitchen and pantry, small and white, were typical of the 1920s era, and while not "off limits" to us, were not visited freely; the door to the kitchen always remained closed. During meals my mother rang a bell under the large walnut dining room table to call a servant from behind the tall decorative screen that shielded the kitchen door. My lasting impression was of spacious rooms, my mother's Chinese rugs on shiny wood floors, comfortable over-stuffed easy chairs and bright sunshine streaming through rows of windows.

My own bedroom, referred to as the children's room, included a small single bed for me and, under the double set of windows, rows of deep walnut shelves where I carefully arranged and rearranged my dolls, tea sets, and other toys. My little brother, then under a year old, had his crib and assorted belongings in one corner. It was a utilitarian nursery rather than anything frilly and pretty, but that, my mother said, would come later.

Of all the rooms in the new apartment I especially liked the bathroom in the master suite. Black marble covered the walls and floor, while the fixtures, including a large ceramic bathtub, were a lovely rich lavender. Several mirrors lined the door and walls and everything seemed bright and sparkling. My bathroom, on the other hand, all white, with small white tiles on the floor, looked dull and uninteresting and, being on the north, felt dark and dreary most of the time. The wash amah usually worked here and here she hung some of our clothes to dry.

Although my parents told me numerous times not to play in the pretty purple bathroom, I paid no attention and even pushed my doll carriage inside. All was well until the day I turned the lock on the door, caught my wrist over the doorknob and broke the beautiful gold bracelet my Grandma Tucker had sent me. I quickly realized I couldn't open the door and, despite my mother's pleading on the other side, couldn't turn the lock back. Then my mother got upset. Boy, Coolie and Amah were called, to no avail. Finally the Coolie was dispatched to the main office for help. The workman who came calmly took the door off its hinges and released me. My mother gave me a long lecture. My father thought it was funny. And I stopped playing in the purple bathroom.

Life at such an apartment was possible only with the help of a staff of Chinese servants. Chang, our "No. 1 House Boy," usually referred to as simply "Boy" served as head butler, housekeeper, manager and chief cook, in effect running the entire household, following the precedent set many years before by the first British to live in Shanghai. He managed the servants, including Amah, the house coolie, the wash amah and the chauffeur. Whatever we might need done, a servant stood ready to do it.

Every day after Daddy left for the office my mother conferred with Chang about meals, as well as any other problem that might arise. They planned the meals for the day so he and the house coolie could go to market and buy what was needed. Foreigners, and certainly most foreign women, who spoke little Chinese, rarely shopped for their own food, finding it difficult to deal with the different vendors of meat, flour, vegetables and other household commodities. Nor was there anything resembling a general grocery store for them to patronize. Chang took over the purchase and preparation of all food, at first under the strict supervision of my mother. Because he was such a good cook, though, she began to leave more and more food decisions up to him—with the understanding that everything must be cooked; we never ate anything raw. We considered ourselves fortunate to have such an excellent and accommodating staff.

For most Americans this was part of the charm of living in Shanghai. From my parents' view it made possible a most enjoyable life style. The danger lay, they thought, in children becoming spoiled. They tried, with varying degrees of success, to avoid this and took special pains to keep my brother and me "in line" and free from the attitude that this sort of relationship with servants often bred. The very nature of the servant set-up, however, encouraged feelings of superiority that were difficult to handle. My days in America would reveal character traits and abilities very different from my contemporaries and I would struggle with learning how to do simple, ordinary, everyday tasks. Although I had an independent spirit, it was often squelched, as I was never allowed to do anything or go anywhere alone. Eventually doing many things on my own became very difficult and, once in America, caused me much confusion and heartache.

My favorite place to play in our apartment was the enclosed veranda. Light and sunny, the tiled floor proved excellent for rolling cars, pushing my doll buggy and building towers with the mah jong set. I usually had my favorite dolls with me. Lulu, whose special eyes opened and closed, had been a fourth birthday present. Daddy loved nicknames and he and I had a long discussion about what to name her. He strongly favored "Maggie." I didn't much like that, and since it was the name of his old girl friend in the States, my mother soon vetoed it. I did like his suggestion of "Lulu," from some song he liked to sing, so it stuck. Amah helped me with Lulu's clothes, seeing that her long lace dresses were washed, starched and carefully ironed. My other favorite, a Chinese boy doll, we agreed to call "Sonny."

The veranda was also where Socko lived. Socko was our canary. Thinking that we needed a pet, and since dogs were not allowed, my father settled on a canary. Once mentioned, it wasn't long before the Coolie appeared with a yellow canary and an elaborate bamboo cage fitted out with swings, perches and whatever else a good canary might desire. It took us days to settle on his name. Other suggestions are forgotten, along with the reasoning behind the selection of "Socko," but "Socko" it was, though his name hardly fit his personality.

Once he was installed, I began to have serious doubts about this bird. He never sang. Seldom, if ever, did he hold forth in song, offering instead only a few weak chirps. Whenever I looked at him he sat on his perch, cocked his head and looked steadily—and silently—back at me. Coolie fed him and cleaned up after him every day, spreading papers underneath the cage, so my contact with this pet was limited to close observation, slipping a canvas cover over his cage at night and removing it the next morning.

One morning after a few weeks, I went out to the veranda to check on Socko and found him lying very still at the bottom of his cage. When my father came out and saw him, I was told to go eat my breakfast, he rang at once for Coolie and that was the last I saw of Socko. We decided not to get another canary, suiting me just fine.

From my fourth birthday to some months past my sixth, the Grosvenor House was home, in many ways providing a very special life for the child that I was.

Amah

"What," asked my mother again, "was the monkey doing?"

I began to cry. I tried to explain that I had been afraid the monkey would *touch* me.

She turned to Amah for clarification.

"Monkee too much jump and run and too much walla walla," said Amah. Translation: The monkey was running and jumping everywhere and there was a lot of confusion and loud noise. "Tuckey no like."

Nobody ever figured out precisely what the monkey did to so upset me and send me sobbing to Amah that I wanted to go home. Parents often hired a monkey for entertainment and the other children at this four-year old's birthday party were having a good time and seemed to accept the monkey and his antics. But I wanted none of him and when my crying didn't stop Amah gathered me up and we left. Still sobbing, I tried to explain to my mother. She said she was embarrassed and would call and apologize. My father laughed and called me a sissy. I knew only that I didn't like monkeys. I calmed down, as usual, with quiet words and expressions of sympathy from Amah.

Her name was "Lah-Nee," but to us she was simply "Amah." To her, at ages one and four years, respectively, my brother and I were—with strangers and when away from home—"Young Master" and "Young Missy." At other times he was "Bir" (like most Chinese she had trouble with the letter "l") and I was "Tuckey." But with respect and affection we always called her "Amah."

When she came to us in that summer of 1938, as we moved into the Grosvenor House apartment, she was, at first, merely one more change in my life. Hired to be Bill's baby amah, I soon came under her supervision as well. She was not my first amah—I had had several. I was especially fond of Wong Inga, my amah during the months we spent in Hankow. I had disliked the Filipino girls who looked after me in Baguio and was scared of the amah at the house on Rue de Lastre. But it did not take long for this new amah to win me over.

A small, thin, immaculate little woman, Amah was probably in her mid-thirties when we first saw her. We learned later that she was married and had at least one son, then around fifteen, and that her family lived in a small village near Shanghai. She wanted to care for children and despite her basic shyness she was curious about the city and undaunted by Westerners. In the face of necessity she set about bringing to her family some badly needed income. Her husband, if he was still living, may have been away in the army, but she never mentioned him. Other relatives sometimes came to visit, staying only for a cup of tea. Once in a while she asked for a day off to go home or to burn *joss* sticks at the family shrine, a part of her religion.

She wore her long black hair in a bun at her neck, and her fine skin and sparkling black eyes along with delicate high cheekbones gave her face real beauty. Her daily uniform was either a long, white cotton *cheongsam* that buttoned at the side in the Chinese fashion, or black silk pants and a white cotton top. She always had on tiny gold earrings; I greatly admired these and begged my mother for holes in my ears, but with no luck. She also wore padded, black cloth house slippers. I was quick to notice that she had regular-sized feet—one of my other amah's feet had been bound and she hobbled slowly and painfully around after me. Nothing, however, stopped this amah, full of energy, from darting here and there, wherever she was needed.

Following the general plan outlined by my mother, a great admirer of the British way of raising children, Amah was responsible for our daily routine. She got me out of bed at seven, served me breakfast at the dining room table with my parents, and then got me dressed for the day. I usually wore a jumper and blouse or a short-sleeved dress with a sweater, socks and cotton house slippers or, when we were going outside, sturdy brown shoes. Never did I even own a pair of long pants or slacks—this was unheard of for little girls like me.

In the mornings I played with my dolls or, if my mother were going shopping or to visit friends, she sometimes took Bill and me with her. Tiffin was at noon and we were always back for tiffin. She ate with us or, if she were going to a luncheon or a bridge party, Amah sat with us.

After tiffin Bill and I went to the nursery for a nap. Then Amah dressed us again for our afternoon visit to the Grosvenor House Garden, the highlight of our day. Every afternoon, weather permitting, our amah and all the other amahs in the building took their charges down to play outside. We loaded our playthings—a ball and a few toys for Bill, a couple of dolls and my tea set—into my doll carriage and headed for the lift. Amah took her large basket with her three-legged low stool and her current piece of knitting, along with other necessities. All amahs were adept at sitting on low stools set up in small circles here and there on the broad, tiled garden terrace, and could knit, gossip, rock a baby buggy and keep an eye on small children all at the same time.

I loved the Garden. It was not a flower garden, for there were none, but rather a space for grass, for fresh air, for walking and for play. We had no playground equipment; no sand boxes, swings, seesaws or slides were to be seen or were expected. Children were to entertain themselves with their own toys. Enclosed on all sides and covering a small city block, with its terraced expanse of grass, shrubbery and young trees, it was above all a safe place for children. The constant cacophony of sound that always emanated from Avenue Joffre, along the Garden's far side, echoed dimly inside the compound's surrounding brick walls and iron gate. Sometimes a curious Chinese or two peered through its iron bars but their vision was restricted by bushes and we were rarely aware of any spectators.

Usually I played with Linda, who lived a floor above us. We would set up a tea party on the wide steps of the terrace, filling the cups with grass or dirt, and serve our dolls. Sometimes two or three other little girls, with their dolls, played with us. I didn't particularly like Linda, who always got her own way, and our friendship ended after she told me she had deliberately slammed their heavy bathroom door on her little sister's fingers.

Children were not supposed to take food into the Garden. Once someone, probably Linda, gave me a piece of candy—a jawbreaker, the first I ever had. Still blissfully sucking on it when we got home, I soon met the wrath of my mother for accepting something "strange" to eat. Never again, both Amah and I were made to understand.

In the absence of wrist watches or clocks, when the shadows from the surrounding tall buildings reached a certain point, all the amahs rose en masse and prepared to leave. Gathering up stools, knitting and various belongings, they rounded up their charges and moved inside, through the black marble foyer with its big potted plants, to the elevators. The Garden now lay free—and quiet—for other residents to enjoy.

The patient Chinese elevator boy always grinned, helped us with our buggy and other paraphernalia and took us up to 303, his lift stopping with a cushioned little jerk. I rushed to ring our doorbell. The foyer, on which opened two lifts, two apartment doors and two stairway doors, frightened me. Dimly lit and somehow forbidding, sounds were distorted and I was glad when Coolie appeared at our door, checking first through the peephole to see who was there, and opened it for us.

Before long my father would get home from the office. He would want to know all we had been up to during the day, so I would report in detail while Amah took an hour or so break before Bill's bath. A daily evening bath was a necessity in this world of countless, invidious germs. We were constantly cautioned to wash our hands after being out and never to put our bare feet on the floor lest germs invade and bring the dread infection known as "Hong Kong Foot"—a very real condition which, once acquired, never seemed to go away. When it was time for my bath I was allowed to play and splash around for a while before being bundled into my soft warm bathrobe and slippers for supper.

One of our parents often sat with Bill and me for our supper. They usually were invited to a friend's house for dinner or went to the Country Club for dinner and a game of bridge or mah jong. Before they left they saw us settled in bed, then Amah got us to sleep. When they returned I always awakened, hearing the sound of the elevator stopping just beyond my room and then the rattle of Daddy's keys at the apartment door. My mother dismissed Amah, checked on us, and I would go back to sleep.

It was about this time that I discovered radio. Our small set sat on the book case between the veranda and the living room and while I was not allowed to operate it, my mother often had it playing, usually tuned to a Shanghai station that broadcast American music. I remember once stopping to listen to a happy song about a little yellow basket that made the whole day much brighter. Two of my favorites were "Over the Rainbow" and "Whistle While You Work."

I was also being introduced to the movies. The first motion picture I was taken to see was "Pinocchio." It was an exciting occasion and we sat in the plush loge of one of Shanghai's most elegant theaters. But my parents had to take me home before the movie ended because I didn't like the large bugs, particularly the crickets that talked and sang, overpowering me from the huge screen and bringing me to tears. After a lapse of a few months they took me to see "Snow White and the Seven Dwarfs" and I was entranced. From then on I begged to go to the movies.

Much of this side of my life was totally foreign to Amah. She could not understand the movies or the song lyrics and I couldn't explain. In fact, verbal communication with Amah was not easy. When we were in the Philippines I forgot all my Chinese and couldn't seem to learn it again. She spoke limited English, mostly the Chinese brand of "Pidgin English" that most servants knew and that I quickly picked up.

Words, though, were not necessary in my relationship with Amah. Nothing that I ever did seemed to draw her wrath or displeasure. When I was being naughty she maneuvered me around until I was behaving. Never did she raise her voice to me. A smile was, for her, all that was needed.

Before long it was to Amah that I turned when things went wrong. Sometimes, though I was not supposed to, I went through the kitchen back to the servants' area and found her in her room. Her room was always neat and clean, with several low wooden stools placed here and there and the narrow bed covered with a bright cotton spread. She would usually be sitting in her low rocking chair during her time off, embroidering or knitting or drinking tea. I would bury my head in her lap, while she patiently smoothed my hair or patted my back. She seemed to know when I had been teased too much, when I had been too "smart" in answering my parents, when I had not been nice to Bill, when too much was expected of me, when I was tired and could push no further. Whatever she said, in Chinese or English, it always calmed me down.

These few short years at Grosvenor House were the happiest of my childhood. In many ways it was Amah who made them so, and when I think of them it is Amah I remember.

Home Leave, 1939

Nineteen thirty-nine was, for many people, a landmark year and not, for everyone, a happy year. In many parts of the world countless hopes and dreams were slipping into the ashes of another world war. The giants of the century were already on stage: Hitler at his peak, Stalin at full steam, Churchill biding his time, and Franklin Roosevelt riding the crest of a nation recovering from the Great Depression and turning toward blue skies and better days. Awaiting an uncertain future, the world seemed to be holding its breath.

My family took home leave in America that spring and by the end of summer was to be directly affected by events across the world. Any U.S. citizen traveling outside of the country could not help but be aware of the international situation and the inherent danger in impending war. That summer forced my parents to alter their usual course and to face difficult decisions. As for me and my small, four-year-old being—1939 introduced me to some of the realities of life.

81

It began with the whooping cough. There were then no shots available to prevent the disease and when I was exposed at a friend's birthday party, I came down with a severe case. Our doctor was called, I was put to bed and Bill and I both were quarantined. Dr. Gardiner visited daily, giving gamma globulin shots to both of us, hoping to ease the disease for me and to allow a milder case for Bill. For weeks into the spring, I was not spared the full force of the whooping cough.

My parents were concerned not only about the whooping cough but also about our scheduled home leave. Our last trip to America had been in 1935. We had been booked for over a year now on the *Empress of Japan*, due to sail for the States in April of 1939. For a while it seemed highly unlikely we could go and they considered rescheduling passage in June on a lesser vessel—not a welcome prospect. Dr. Gardiner finally agreed to the trip as planned, saying I was over the worst, and the ship's authorities approved our passage provided I remained in quarantine in our stateroom.

By the time we reached Honolulu the quarantine had expired and I felt well enough to take a break from the ship and go ashore. In a day or so we set sail with the customary aloha sendoff—a band, hula dancing and miles of colored streamers tossed between ship and shore. It was an exciting time to be traveling.

We docked in San Francisco in early May—three weeks after we had left Shanghai—and checked into the St. Francis Hotel. The next day we boarded a train for Detroit, where we picked up the new, two-door Plymouth my father had arranged to have waiting for us. It bore a special license tag indicating it was under lease until August 31st, when it would be returned to a dealer. We then drove down through Ohio and West Virginia and across Virginia to La Crosse, or as Daddy always called it, "Lay-Cross."

We arrived in La Crosse at dusk on a soft May evening when the air felt like velvet and smelled of roses and honeysuckle. As we drove up the hill and turned the last corner of our long journey, I felt like we had indeed reached the end of the rainbow.

At the top of the hill some children were playing. When Daddy stopped the car they ran up to us.

"Hey, Uncle Jake!" one of them shouted.

This was, I knew, my cousin Betty Ran, three years older than I. After a few words with Daddy and "Aunt Polly" and a glance at me, she announced that she would run on ahead and tell everyone we had come. Blowing the horn, Daddy drove slowly down the road and parked in front of a big white house. A group of my mother's relatives poured out the front door to greet us.

After everyone had been hugged and Bill and I closely inspected, we all sat down in the living room. Bill went around and rearranged ashtrays on the tables, ignoring the adults around us. I leaned on the edge of my mother's chair, suddenly shy with so many strange people.

This was the home of my Aunt Beck, my mother's half-sister and much older than she. Her husband Jim, their daughter Agnes and her husband Charlie and their daughter Betty Randolph lived here. My mother's sister Nancy, who taught school in Roanoke, spent her vacations here; during our visit she was staying up the street at an aunt's but would come down each morning. Aunt Beck's would serve as a kind of headquarters for us while we were in Virginia and it was this part of the family that I came to know best.

At some point over the next day or so my mother decided that I was not well. Since I was running a fever, I was put to bed. "Peaked" was one thing they called me. The young doctor who came—an old friend of my mother's—called me "one of the most nervous children" he had ever seen. He gave me a shot and prescribed two weeks of quiet and bed rest.

Family and friends from all over appeared at Aunt Beck's house for a visit, some coming up to take a peek at me. Most of the time they sat in lawn chairs out in the front yard under the shade trees. I perched on the end of the bed and looked out the window at all the activity, discreetly observing my many relatives. In the morning a breeze lifted the sheer lace curtains, but by afternoon it grew hot and they hung limp at the screens. Every so often someone brought me something to eat or drink—urging it on me "for your own good"—and occasionally my Aunt Nancy sat and read to me. I missed Amah and wanted to go back home.

Among the visiting relatives was a cousin, a year or so younger than I. She was not a happy visitor. My mother came upstairs, insisting that I lend her my doll to play with. This, she said, would be the polite thing to do. I protested at giving up Lulu, my long-time favorite doll, but I grudgingly let her go. After the company had gone my mother brought her back upstairs. As I took hold of her I looked down at a dirty dress and a face that had black smudges and two blank holes—Lulu's special eyes had been punched into her head. I was devastated. With a terrible feeling I turned over and closed my own eyes. My mother promised me a beautiful new doll—a Shirley Temple, very popular then—but I never liked it and longed for Lulu.

After I was allowed up we began our own round of visits, mostly to family. It was hard for them, adults and children alike, to realize that I had not grown up as they had, on a Virginia farm, and that my China background was different even from my father's experience. No one seemed to understand, too, that they were all strangers to me, even if they were my relatives.

84

We spent several days at Aunt Mamie's, one of my father's five sisters. She and her husband, Bill Tanner, lived in a big old Virginia farmhouse near Palmer Springs, where many of my father's relatives lived. Tall, dark green boxwood bushes, their sharp, musky scent filling the summer air, lined the walk leading up to their front porch, making a great place to play and hide.

Aunt Mamie's house was always full of people. My Grandma Tucker stayed for weeks at a time and other relatives visited, among them Aunt Fannie, Daddy's oldest sister, a redhead who was married four times—her several children were all grown, with their own families. Others came down from Washington to see us. These included Aunt Rosa and Aunt Bertha, with her daughters Peggy and Joyce, closer to my age, and Uncle Albert, Daddy's brother.

A half-dozen or so colored people—so different from the Chinese servants I was used to—came up to the house every day to help in the kitchen, cooking huge meals for noon dinners. The long dining room table was covered with platters of fried chicken—their necks wrung only hours before—smoked ham, fresh corn, butter beans, string beans, mashed potatoes, sliced tomatoes, watermelon and peach pickle, strawberry and damson preserves, hot biscuits, hot rolls, buttermilk and sweet milk, iced tea, cake, pie and sometimes homemade ice cream. There were often so many people, family and visitors, that we ate in two shifts, with the children sitting at a smaller side table.

My father's family loved to tease, and Bill and I were prime targets. Aunt Mamie's husband was a large, genial man who meant no harm, but he had somehow had a big toe cut off and, despite my protests, he always removed his sock and shoe to show us his maimed foot and missing toe. One of their sons had unfortunately had his arm caught in a piece of farm machinery, cutting it off above the elbow; this, too, over even louder protests, was displayed for us. My father was the main culprit in all this, always bringing up the subject and insisting to my mother that "reality" was good for us.

We also visited Daddy's sister Willie and her husband, who had no children, on their farm. And we stayed a week with Mama's brother Holmes, his wife Mary and their two children at their cottage on the Chesapeake Bay. Other relatives like my Uncle Thornton also visited us there.

During July we rented a cottage at Virginia Beach. It was then barely a small town, with little commercial development and only summer cottages near the beach. I loved the sand and the ocean, and except for one bout with a bad sunburn, fared better than I had all summer.

With the approach of August my parents made plans to start back to China. Our last few days we spent at Aunt Beck's, packing and getting all in order. We also celebrated several family birthdays, including my fifth.

We left for California amid the usual bevy of relatives, including my great grandmother Bowen, then in her nineties and positive, as always, that she would never lay eyes on us again. Our car was packed to the ceiling. Daddy, who did all of the driving, and Mama sat in the front seat, while Bill stood in the middle between them, watching all three thousand miles of the road in front of us. I sat in the right back seat. To my left were stacked boxes, suitcases, clothes, toys—everything there was no room for in the trunk. Aunt Beck said later that when we pulled out all she could see of me was the top of my head, squeezed in next to a pile of stuff she feared would topple over on me before we had gone a mile.

Grandma Tucker and several others drove over from Palmer

Springs to see us off. She hugged me and closed a dime in my fist, whispering in my ear for me to count every white horse I saw— she'd give me a penny for each one. I watched carefully for a day or so, but then I began to wonder just how she would actually get those pennies to me. Besides, I had only seen one white horse, so I stopped counting.

We followed Route 40 across West Virginia and on toward the Mississippi River. Like most highways then, it was a two-lane winding road that went through small towns as well as cities. Farther west there were other route numbers but never very good roads, with frequent detours. We usually made around three hundred miles a day.

We drove for days, the pattern always the same. Leaving early in the morning after breakfast, we stopped around noon at a diner or cafe for lunch. While we waited for our order we were usually served soda crackers and ice-cold tomato juice—since the weather was hot and there was no air conditioning, this tasted good and I looked forward to it. I also hoped for a juke box in the lunchroom so I could get Daddy to play some records. My first choice was always Frankie Carle's "Sunrise Serenade." Some places had elaborate juke boxes with swirls of color and lights that moved around inside. Sometimes I got to go up to the box myself, put the nickel in the slot, shove it in, watch the record slowly slide out and the needle fall, and then hear the room fill with music.

Every afternoon around five o'clock we began to look for a good place to spend the night. There were, of course, no motels, and not many "tourist courts" that looked clean enough to suit my mother. Mostly we stayed at a town's hotel, if it had one, or at one of the big houses that had signs out for overnight guests. Sometimes it would get dark and we'd still be driving; once in some small midwestern town we asked a policeman for help and he led us to a tourist house on the highway.

Whenever we stopped, especially at a hotel, Daddy would order up some ice and water and pour himself a "stiff drink." Then we'd go down to the dining room for supper. Some places were better than others; in most I remember the cool starched sheets on my bed. The next morning we'd start the same routine again.

Finally we reached San Francisco and the St. Francis Hotel. Though it meant nothing to me, my parents were anxious to hear news about Europe. With no car radio and few newspapers along the way they lacked up-to-date news. I could tell the next day when Daddy returned from talking to BAT officials that something serious was going on. After several phone calls, with snatches of conversation about Germany and Poland, world war and the Japanese, my parents made their decision. They sent a telegram to Aunt Beck and before the car had been completely unpacked, we packed up again and left San Francisco, heading back east.

Instead of boarding an ocean liner we were returning to Virginia. Worried about taking his family to China with a world war threatening, my father was following company advice and leaving us in America. He would drive us back to La Crosse and then catch a train to California in time to board ship for China. My mother, upset at the idea of being separated from him, nevertheless realized that they hadn't much choice. The three of us would wait in the States, hoping that things abroad would calm down so that we could follow in a few weeks.

Driving much longer each day, pushing against the tight time schedule, we again pulled into La Crosse. Within hours Daddy caught a train back to California.

It was September. We spent nearly three months in La Crosse, caught up in the family life at Aunt Beck's. My attachment to them became so strong that when we finally left to go back to China I cried for hours with homesickness.

With the Far East situation appearing quieter, the BAT booked passage for us back to Shanghai in December. My mother, with Bill and me in tow, caught the train for the two-day trip from Richmond to Chicago, where her uncle and his wife met us and took us to their apartment for the night.

The next day we boarded an express train for Los Angeles. There we stayed at the Biltmore Hotel until our ship sailed two days later. By then my mother had met other BAT wives who were returning on the same liner. The voyage itself was uneventful, but she was seasick and we remained in our cabin much of the time. Christmas was spent on the ship and a few days afterward we reached Shanghai.

I was glad to leave the ship, relieved the long journey was over at last. Among my memories was a painful one of Bill and me standing alone at a Christmas Day gathering in the ship's large lounge, looking at a beautiful Christmas tree surrounded with presents—not one of which was labeled for either of us. Adults and the ship's purser who noticed us were most apologetic at such an oversight. The purser tried to remedy the situation, appearing at our cabin with gifts, but I never touched the tea set he brought me.

My mother, overwhelmed by the burden of traveling alone with two small children and by her own ill health, also had memories of that trip. One was Bill's whisper to her after Daddy boarded ship in Shanghai and then left the cabin for a moment to see about our luggage. "Mommy," he said, "who was that man?"

Back at 303 Grosvenor House we greeted Amah and slipped into our familiar routine. As the old year faded, we welcomed a promising new one—1940.

At School

$\mathcal{I}$n August of 1940, after my sixth birthday, my parents began talking to me about school—first grade. There was no preschool or kindergarten for me or my friends; those who were six years old simply began with first grade. They enrolled me at the American School where several boys and girls I knew would be going. It was a new experience, but I remember no particular anxiety or fear of school. I reasoned then, as I would on many other occasions to come, that if this was what one did at my age and all the other children did it, then I could do it, too.

The Shanghai American School was a private institution organized and run by a board of American missionaries and businessmen. Tuition was charged by the month. All Americans were welcome and while children of other nationalities were also enrolled, early elementary pupils were mostly American.

The school was located on a large campus three or four miles from Grosvenor House on Avenue Petain. The first and second grades were housed not in the main S.A.S. building, a large, three-story brick structure, but in a small house on the edge of the grounds near an entrance through the bamboo fence surrounding the campus. It looked like a small cottage set down in a clump of green trees and bushes and would always remind me of the little house in "Hansel and Gretel," except there was no witch and this was a friendly little cottage.

Every morning before they went to the office Daddy and Mo Ling would drive me out to the school. Mo Ling always took me inside the fence and saw me safely to the front door. There we lined up to go inside.

The six-year-olds filed into the first grade room on the left—around twenty of us—and a similar number of second graders into the classroom on the right. My teacher was Mrs. Nisbit, a middle-aged American lady with a soft voice and a nice smile. I liked her quiet ways and her look of calm and being in charge. She never seemed to get very excited about anything.

I liked my assigned chair and the low table, which seated six. I already knew my numbers from playing solitaire and dominoes with Daddy, but I expected to learn to read and write. Instead of letters and numbers, though, we spent a good deal of time learning our colors and how to handle crayons. Mostly we colored different shapes: circles, squares, triangles and rectangles. I could stay inside the lines but some of the others had trouble keeping their crayons from going outside the lines and some of their work looked to me like scribbling. I decided that reading and writing surely would come, so I tried to do my best with the colors. At the teacher's direction we each made a booklet of several pages of colored shapes to take home to our parents.

We sang a lot. One song was "Old MacDonald's Farm"—we all liked the "E-I-E-I-O." We also memorized a short poem that began

"There was a little mouse that lived at our house, and what can be the use of him is more than I can see. . . ." I had never seen a real mouse but I learned the poem and practiced saying it for my parents—giving my father a good laugh every time he heard it.

At recess, outside on the playground beside the little house, we all played games together. We usually played "Drop the Handkerchief," "Ring Around the Rosie," and "The Farmer in the Dell." Then we would stop and eat the snack we had been told to bring from home. Mine was always a small dry peanut butter and jelly sandwich that Boy or Amah fixed for me. After we lined up in the kitchen for a drink of water we settled back down in the classroom. Sometimes our teacher would read us an interesting story.

One morning all the girls were lined up and marched across campus to the "Big Building," where the infirmary was located. Here we were to get our "physicals," a dreaded procedure required of everyone. Dark tales had come down to us from a few second graders as to what awaited us and possible consequences. We assumed that if we didn't pass we would be immediately sent home—for good. We were all a little uneasy. Once there, a nurse came in and told us to "remove your dress and shoes" and line up again. There we waited, a gaggle of giggling six-year-olds, clad in white socks and ruffled petticoats, ready to be "examined." All of us passed, our fears were eased and we got to stay in school.

Our school day finished shortly after noon. Amah was always waiting for me just inside the bamboo fence. We would ride home together in a ricksha. Each day a ricksha coolie she knew would get permission to wait for her at the Grosvenor House servants' entrance and would drive her to school in plenty of time to meet me.

This was an especially nice ricksha. Its large wheels were always swept clear of mud or debris of any kind and its trim polished a bright shiny black. Its soft, cushioned seat and back were covered in immaculate white starched cotton. The foot piece was also kept clean, as was the collapsible black roof that was raised over the passenger if it should rain. I thought the ricksha coolie himself looked cleaner than most. He wore a white cotton shirt, black pants and sandals on his feet instead of going barefoot. When Amah and I came out of the gate he always moved the ricksha up closer, nodded at me and said "How do, Little Missy."

I loved riding in the ricksha. I would get in first and then Amah. Sometimes I held my breath because the ricksha tipped far back while we got settled in the seat—but I knew Amah wouldn't let me fall out. Then the coolie would pick up the long handles, stand between them and start running down the street, his sandals making a *slap, slap* sound as his feet hit the pavement, the ricksha rolling steadily behind him.

Riding in the ricksha Amah and I could see everything. We began on Avenue Petain, a wide, pretty, quiet street with grass and trees along the sides. There was usually very little traffic except for one or two other rickshas carrying my classmates, and here and there an automobile. After several blocks we turned into Avenue Joffre where there were trams, many more cars and rickshas, and lots of people. The coolie would turn off when we reached Rue Cardinal Mercier and slow down at the entrance to the Grosvenor House. Here the Chinese watchman emerged from his guard house, looked at us and smiled, waving us on into the compound. The wind always blew fiercely here, sweeping around us as we turned and followed the wide drive curving to the front entrance. Sometimes I would look up and wave at my mother and Bill watching for us from our dining room window.

Amah would pay the coolie the fare, along with some *cumsha* (a tip or generous extra money paid for good service) that Daddy had given her for the ricksha ride, remind him to meet her again the next day, and off he would go. Inside, waiting for me would be tiffin, usually my favorite beef tea and rice and other good things like gingerbread that Boy cooked for us.

Then I would tell Mama and Bill what fun things I had done at school and what I had learned—which usually wasn't much. But the best part of going to school was riding home with Amah in the shiny, rolling ricksha.

One Sunday Morning

"Where are we going today?" I asked as I stood with my parents and little brother on the steps of the Grosvenor House entrance, waiting for Mo Ling to bring the car. As he pulled up, the doorman stepped forward to open the doors for us, my father getting in the front seat today, my mother, Bill and I settling into the back, with me beside the window. It was a cold, sunny day and I had on my new winter coat with its matching velvet hat and muff; they made me feel very grown-up. We were going, said my father, to the BAT factory down in Hongkew "to check on things."

As a six-year old I had few chances to go on such a long ride. There was always a lot to see anywhere in Shanghai and I looked forward to these family excursions. Sometimes we went to the Columbia Country Club where we would walk around the grounds, inspect the swimming pool and tennis courts or watch the pin boys at work in the bowling alley. Then we ate tiffin on the large veranda. For dessert Bill and I always ordered ice cream. It usually came in a Dixie cup—a small, round, cardboard container with a tiny wooden spoon—and was almost always vanilla. Occasionally we could get a block of striped ice cream of three flavors—a stripe of brown (chocolate), a stripe of white (vanilla) and a stripe of bright pink (strawberry). For us, any ice cream was a treat.

Sometimes we drove out Hungjao Road, past the wealthy estates into the country. Here, only a few miles from the city, the land was level, green, suddenly rural—and somehow bleak. Peasants, some of them yoked to crude plows, worked in the swampy rice paddies. Here and there bamboo huts perched on small, bare clearings of mud. Everything seemed primitive and stark. Flowers grew somewhere near Shanghai, but not here. Dotting the countryside were high grassy mounds, much taller than a man; these were ancestors' graves, some of them centuries old. There was little traffic and our car seemed very small on the straight two-lane road, surrounded by flat open land. We never went far because the pavement was bumpy to drive on and would soon end—and because my mother was always afraid of bandits roaming the countryside, ready to attack any foreigner.

Today, though, we turned down Avenue Joffre to Avenue Edward VII and the Bund. Once beyond the quieter French Concession, traffic became heavy and loud. Driving on the left side of the street, we crept along beside all kinds of vehicles, from Cadillacs to clanging street cars, bicycles and handcarts to wheelbarrows and rickshas and even a wagon pulled by oxen.

At times Mo Ling had to stop until a traffic jam ahead of us cleared. Since there were few stop lights, Sikhs directed traffic, standing in towers built on the small concrete islands at each wide intersection and motioning their long arms toward the cars. Pedestrians, oblivious to directions, pushed and shoved to get across streets, yelling and calling out to those around them.

Ricksha coolies wandered here and there, in between automobiles, seeking a fare. Other coolies, unable to see ahead, their necks bent under bamboo poles bearing heavy loads, shouted and chanted as they trotted along, warning people to get out of their way.

Street stalls offered hot rice, fried noodles, meat wrapped in pastry, pickles, hundred-year-old eggs and other Chinese delicacies—all forbidden to me since they came off the street. Hawkers called out their goods: bolts of bright red silk, bamboo bird cages, painted red paper dragons, carved boxes, crickets chirping in tiny reed baskets, lucky jade pieces, live chickens, long, skinny opium pipes. . . . Customers everywhere jabbered at the top of their voices, haggling over money, trying to reach a mutually acceptable price or trade. The entire downtown district resonated with discordant sound, blaring horns, harsh shouting and frantic activity.

Down cobblestone alleyways women with babies strapped to their bodies tended small cook stoves that sat on the ground. Swarms of children, many almost naked, ran in and out of dark doorways, around street stalls and up and down steps. Barbers shaved their customers on tall stools in the middle of the alley. Here and there beside small tables sat "scholars," educated men who wrote letters, documents, various notices and announcements for their customers—or read them aloud upon request—for a fee. On rickety tables leaning against narrow storefronts old men with straggly gray beards and heavy eyelids played mah jong, their steaming cups of tea and long pipes within easy reach. Pungent smells—some perfumed, fragrant and spicy, some reeking of sewage and garbage—clung to the streets. Fresh air was as foreign as many of the shoppers.

Beggars huddled along the sidewalks, arms reaching up to anyone passing by, pleading for money. I always hated to look at them but they were everywhere. Among them always were the maimed, the blind and the crippled, some of their physical deformities deliberately caused by their own family at an early age. Some with no legs scooted along on their small wheeled platforms. All gave an impression of grinding dirt, with filthy hands and faces and soiled, ragged clothing. Children with diseased eyes, facial scabs and runny noses, their arms and legs wrapped in strips of faded rags, grabbed at the coattails and sleeves of passing foreigners, blocking their paths. In shrill, sing-song voices they begged for money. I felt very sorry for them. But Westerners, even children, were warned not to give money to even one or they would be surrounded by every beggar in sight.

We soon reached the Bund. Called Shanghai's main street, it ran right along the bank of the river, only a strip of grass in some places separating it from the wharves and the water. The broad thoroughfare, wide enough for a row of cars to be parked across its center, dominated downtown. Children were always reminded to watch for the Hong Kong and Shanghai Bank—two huge bronze lions guarded its entrance and rubbing their paws brought you good luck. Once, when we were walking along there, Daddy let me rub a paw so I, too, could have good luck.

Today, as usual, the harbor teemed with all kinds of ships. A gleaming white luxury liner—one of the Canadian "Empress" line—was docked at one pier. Maritime white was a color alien to the Shanghai waterfront and it seemed spotlighted in the harbor. Except for the foreign vessels everything seemed gray, brown, black or dark red, dingy and drab. Further downriver commercial vessels loaded with tea, rice, bamboo, cotton and teakwood, were getting ready to sail out to the world. Other ships carried silks and linens, porcelain and fine china, rugs, curios, ivory and jade. Today I could see, too, the military ships; out in mid-harbor were Japanese battleships, British gunboats and American naval ships, all more prominent since the recent fighting.

Customs tenders and small municipal launches moved around the river, while Chinese junks of all sizes sailed up and down, handling local trade. Near the river banks drifted dozens of sampans, small wooden fishing boats, each with its resident family on board. There were few modern Chinese vessels, though—no Chinese navy, no fleet of Chinese ocean-going commercial ships.

Toward the north, at the end of the Bund and flowing into the Whangpoo, was Soochow Creek. It, too, was lined with masses of sampans, looking almost like a floor had been laid from one side of the creek to the other. The whole area teemed with people of all ages. Many were said to spend their entire lives on these boats, never setting foot on land.

On the sampans' narrow decks women cooked rice and fish and brewed pots of tea on small, make-shift burners. Drab articles of clothing and other laundry, washed in the creek, hung on short lines, dipping close to the muddy water. The same creek water served for drinking and for washing people—and for the disposal of sewage and garbage. Lines of small children, tied to each other by a rope around their waists, from the youngest toddler up to the seven- or eight-year-old in charge, darted here and there, some perilously close to deck's edge. A few men fished in the creek with short poles. Others squatted on deck, sipping tea, smoking a pipe or throwing their fingers out in age-old gambling games. People shouted at each other against background sounds of street traffic, ships' horns, children's shrieks, coolies' chants and, from somewhere, the wail of a Chinese violin.

Traffic crossed the Creek at several places at the north end of the Bund. We headed for the Garden Bridge into Hongkew, one of the busiest intersections in the city. On this particular morning, as had been the case since the latest hostilities, Japanese soldiers patrolled outside a pill box at the end of the bridge. Dressed in full uniform, including their funny-looking white leggings, they held rifles with bayonets out in front of them wherever they went.

As we approached the bridge, Mo Ling slowed to a stop. Beside us were several Chinese pedestrians. Each was stopped by a soldier, ordered to show his pass and then to remove his hat and bow in the direction of His Imperial Majesty, the Emperor of Japan. The sense of power that these Japanese held over every Chinese hung in the air around every coolie and threatened even the more affluent who of necessity passed that way.

Daddy handed Mo Ling our papers and when one guard came over to our car, he glanced inside and, seeing Americans, waved us ahead. Hongkew, despite being a part of the International Settlement, was now under Japanese control. As more of them had moved in, more Westerners had moved out. It was clear the Japanese dominated the area. It was not so clear when they might expand still further and fighting would break out again.

We soon drove through the entrance of the Thorburn Roads branch of the BAT's Yee Tsoong Tobacco Company. The grounds were immaculate—every scrap of litter removed by factory coolies. Heavy gates enclosed the compound with its large brick buildings. Surrounding it were high concrete walls, the tops of which were thickly studded with broken pieces of glass sticking straight up, ready to deter any intruder. Chinese watchmen always stood on guard at the gates.

Some of the head staff—both Russian and Chinese—greeted us

at the entrance to the main building, bowing to my mother and smiling at Bill and me. My father went ahead to his office to see to business. Although British and Americans in the company got most of Saturday and Sundays off, the cigarette machines worked at their normal capacity and operations continued as usual with the Chinese workers.

One of the head Chinese, speaking English, led us into the cavernous main factory to watch the workers make cigarettes. The roar of the huge clanking machines echoed around us so we could barely hear each other talk. I loved the warm rich brown aroma of tobacco that always washed over me in this building. For a few minutes we watched as hundreds of cigarettes rolled out of one machine. A smiling worker, eager to show off for us, caught a few dozen in a paper bag for Daddy to take home. These were *cumsha*; they would fill the silver cigarette box on our coffee table and be given as tips or gifts to various visitors and servants. Sometimes a worker would wrap up a package of loose tobacco for him to take home; this was to go into the cut glass jar that sat beside his chair, close at hand when he was ready to fill his pipe.

We stepped into the dining room, declined an offer of tea and walked on outside to the vegetable garden, a large area devoted to growing vegetables and fruit. In season some would be sent home to Boy to be cooked for our meals. Everything always had to be cooked, even the produce grown within the compound and cared for by the gardener. The Chinese use of human fertilizer, totally unacceptable to Westerners, was difficult to completely guard against. We ate nothing uncooked—no lettuce, strawberries, tomatoes, apples—nothing raw.

Daddy's business done, we were called back to his office. After saying a proper thank you to our escort, we were ushered out to the car. We did not stay for lunch on every visit and on this day Daddy had suggested we stop for tiffin at one of the large hotels on the Bund.

I didn't remember ever being at the Cathay Hotel and was awed by its size and British elegance. It was early for Sunday luncheon, with few guests around. The head boy showed us into a large, wood-paneled dining room filled with tables dressed in stiff white linen tablecloths, heavy, ornate silverware and sparkling crystal, with centerpieces of fresh flowers. Three Chinese waiters rushed over to help us with menus, to bring ice water and drinks for my parents and to keep an eye on Bill and me—children were not, as usual, particularly welcome.

What we had to eat I don't remember—perhaps a fancy brunch. What made the meal memorable for me was my order of hot chocolate. When my mother suggested that I might like some, I quickly agreed. It arrived, hot and steaming, in a heavy, tall, pewter chocolate-pot with a side handle that stuck straight out. At once a waiter filled my cup with the dark, creamy chocolate. I drank it slowly, spilled not one drop and was even allowed a second cup. It was so delicious.

Our meal over, we left the dining room, now filling with guests. In the main lobby we walked beside the hotel shops, their display windows filled with beautiful pieces of expensive jade, carved ivory and hand-embroidered silk gowns. Then we sat down for a few minutes to look around and watch the people while our car was called. Mo Ling drove us home up Nanking Road, past the Race Course to Bubbling Well Road and over to Rue Cardinal Mercier and the Grosvenor House.

It had been a bright, sunlit, happy morning. It turned out to be the last such family outing before we again had to leave Shanghai. I would long remember the ride with my father, the visit to an interesting new place—and one lovely, special chocolate pot.

Leaving

$\mathcal{I}$ leaned my head against the doorway of our living room, closed my eyes and felt the sadness creep over me. From the radio came the strains of Tommy Dorsey's theme song, signaling the end of his program and time for the five o'clock news that my mother listened to every evening. Her knitting lay waiting on the table by her chair. Bill was rolling his cars back and forth out on the veranda floor. Amah was in the kitchen drinking her tea. Coolie had just come in to turn on the lights, including the floor lamp beside my father's chair. The card table sat waiting for his and my nightly game—sometimes we played dominoes and sometimes double solitaire.

Only one more day and I would be gone from all this. Gone from home. I felt the familiar tightening in my stomach. I knew we had to go. Not only did my father say so but, as the radio had so often reported, so did the United States government.

It had been less than a year since we had returned from our long leave in the States. The international situation, particularly conditions in the Far East, had not improved. The U.S. State Department had delayed as long as possible the decision to evacuate American women and children from China but, unable now to guarantee their safety, they issued the order in October of 1940. There were clear signs that war might come: the Japanese had signed a military and economic pact with Germany and Italy, the U.S. had recently refused to renew a trade treaty with Japan, the Chinese were still trying to regain their conquered lands, and actions elsewhere in the Pacific had intensified an underlying fear and suspicion of the Japanese.

Shanghai's three thousand or so Americans reacted with mixed feelings to the announcement. Some could not believe that the powerful United States government could not protect its nationals anywhere in the world. Some were shocked that their government could even think of such a move; would it continue to protect their financial and philanthropic interests? Some saw no danger and declined to send home wives and children. Others understood that the reasons for such dire diplomatic action had been seething beneath the surface of Shanghai life for months: the encroachment of the Japanese on more areas of the city, their assumption of more civic control, and their arrogance in either ignoring or deliberately baiting U.S. citizens. Now that the order had come, most American women and children prepared once again for evacuation.

The first effect of this announcement on my own life was my removal from school. With the evacuation notice my parents decided that for the two weeks or so remaining until our departure, it would be better for me to stop school and stay home. So my name, along with many others, was withdrawn from the school rolls at the end of October.

Most Americans in Shanghai planned for departure as soon as

possible. We were booked on the crowded *Empress of Asia*, one of the luxury ships of the Canadian-Pacific line, expected to call in November. A large number of American BAT wives and children were scheduled to leave on it, so my mother would be traveling with some close friends.

Already our apartment had been torn up for days as BAT coolies came in to pack our furniture. Around a dozen sturdy wood packing crates of varying sizes were built. Each was numbered and stenciled on the sides with our name, along with the address of the BAT affiliate in Richmond, Virginia. They were to follow us on a slower cargo vessel.

Being sent to America, along with some of our household goods, were the Chinese treasures my parents had collected over the years: the tall, carved screen with its colored, inlaid gem stones; two carved teakwood cedar chests; two Chinese rugs; a prized tea set; the bamboo china set; dozens of linen tablecloths; two old Chinese tapestries; small inlaid tables; ivory figurines. . . This afternoon the apartment looked almost bare. Not packed were the wooden junk that sat on our living room mantle; a large framed, tinted photograph of Mama, Bill and me; the walnut dining room suite; the living room sofa and chairs; beds and all my toys and dolls, still sitting in their places on the shelves in my bedroom. After all, my mother explained, Daddy would still be living here. Besides, she said, it wouldn't be too long before we would be coming back. This I didn't believe.

As three o'clock approached on the afternoon of our departure, Bill and I got our coats on and the servants gathered in the foyer to tell us goodby. We shook hands with each. Then we got to Amah. Both of us reached for her and began to cry. She had her arms around us and, as my father began calling us, urged us toward the door. But we clung to her, sobbing, until suddenly she pulled herself away, turned and hurried, grim-faced toward the kitchen. I stared after her as my mother grabbed my hand, Daddy picked up Bill and we pushed out the door to the elevator.

Outside, Mo Ling and the car were waiting, our luggage already in the trunk. The day was cold and dreary. The wind whipped through the compound and the sky looked like a bowl of dark gray clouds turned upside down, with only a tiny rim of rose and gold around the horizon. I had never seen the sky look like this and watched it out of the car window as we drove to the Bund and the jetty where our ship was docked.

On board Daddy led us first to our stateroom and then to join BAT friends in the lounge. Several children were on deck, running around, playing games, so I went outside. But I didn't feel like playing.

It was almost dark now. The lights of the Bund were shining brightly across the way. I stood at the railing and looked down into the dark, treacherous water, watching their reflection. Something deep inside of me was hurting.

In a few minutes Daddy came over and leaned down to talk to me.

"Be a good girl," he said. "Help Mommy look after Bill. And try not to cry."

I nodded. My throat was so tight I couldn't speak. He held out his hand, I laid mine in it and we shook hands.

When visitors were told to leave the ship, we all walked around to the gangplank, and before I knew it Daddy was gone. My mother had lifted her head and put on her brave smile. But I knew it would not last long.

I looked down once again at the lights shimmering in the dark water. When would I ever see my father again?

The *Empress of Asia* sounded its deep, resonant warning whistle and slowly pulled away from the pier, heading down the Whangpoo to the Yangtze and the China Sea. The low, reverberating blast of the horn, repeated over and over, hurt my ears.

Down in our cabin I went over to the small stainless steel lavatory with the faucets that folded up so neatly into such a nice little compartment. Again and again I opened and closed it, fascinated by how it all fit together.

Soon it was time for dinner and we went down to the dining room. It was elegant to look at and the food smelled delicious, but I wasn't hungry.

Back in our cabin it was at last time for bed. I curled up into a tight little ball by myself in the upper bunk. I was determined not to cry. But I longed desperately for Amah. And for home.

Every so often on this first evening out, while we were still near the China coast, I could hear the ship's fog horn sounding, lonely and sad. Saying goodbye.

Tientsin, 1931

Because China beckoned and because he [My father, Jake] had the courage to take a chance, he changed the course of his life—and, of course, the lives of his children.

BRITISH CIGARETTE COMPANY, LIMITED.
(INCORPORATED UNDER THE COMPANIES ORDINANCES OF HONGKONG.)

HEAD OFFICE:- SHANGHAI.

SIR H. CUNLIFFE OWEN, BART. CHAIRMAN

C. G. NEWSON, SECRETARY

June 12th 1928

...ETTE" SHANGHAI
... SHANGHAI
...ETTE" HANKOW
... HANKOW
...RETTE" TIENTSIN

IN YOUR REPL... ...TO FILE NO.

... ma,

Since writing to ...

... have settled down ...

... or practically so ...

... is being asked all ...

... is Chang Tso Lin dead or ...

... seems to know definite...

... gners here are about e...

... in opinion, some of th...

... who are just as ...

... official circles will ...

... ...ding that he is dead

... ...po are sitting ...

... ...ed for trouble but the ...

... ...trouble as the Chine...

... next month.

To Rosa...
from ...
Jak...

They were married, my parents, on a beautiful summer afternoon in the garden at her sister Beck's home, beneath the rose arbor amid a profusion of flowers.

Mrs. Holmes Conrad Harrison

announces the marriage of her daughter

Evelyn Byrd

to

Mr. William Jacob Tucker, Jr.

on Thursday, July the second

nineteen hundred and thirty-one

La Crosse, Virginia

At Home

after August the fifteenth

Shanghai, China

They were booked, first class, by the "Dollar Steam-ship Line (Orient and Around the World)" on the SS *President Harrison*.

. . . they were singled out as having been married the shortest time. . . . a special cake, with one candle, was brought to their table and sliced with the sword of one of the naval officers present.

MESSAGE

MESSAGE

Harrison
Shanghia china

ON BOARD S.S. PRESIDENT
EN ROUTE TO

S. S. "PRESIDENT HARRISON"
W. H. Weaver, Jr. Commander.

"FAREWELL TO OUR DEPARTING GUESTS"
DINNER

Green Onions	California Oyster Cocktail	
Foie Gras Canape	Olives Stuffed with Anchovies	
	Oeufs Farcis	Salted Nuts
		Hearts of Celery
Potage Minestrone	Soup	
		Consomme Froid en Tasse

Fish
Poached Filets of Barracuda, Hollandaise

Entrees
Grenadines of Beef, Financiere
Breaded Veal Cutlets, Portugaise
Fried Fresh Mushrooms on Buttered Toast

Roasts
Prime Rib & Sirloin of Beef, Horseradish Sauce
Young Philadelphia Capon, Sauce Gibier
Baked Southern Ham Wine Sauce

Vegetables
Globe Artichokes au Beurre
Roast Potatoes
Lima Beans in Parsley Sauce
Boiled New Potatoes
Assorted Cold Cuts with Potato Salad

Salad
Combination with French Dressing

Dessert
New York Plum Pudding, Hard Sauce
French Pastry   Plain & Fruit Cake
Hot Mince Pie
Angel Cake
Cheese: Ice Cream   Sugar Wafers
Gorgonzola   McLaren's   Camembert
Fresh Apricots   Toasted Crackers
Cluster Raisins   Watermelon   Fresh Plums   Seedless Grapes
Mixed Nuts   Chinese Cumquats
After Dinner Mints
Cafe Noir

Thursday July, 30th, 1931.

ALOHA. OE.

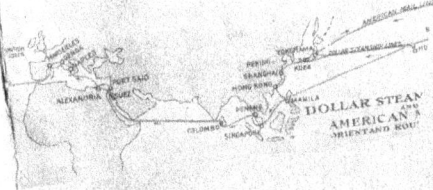

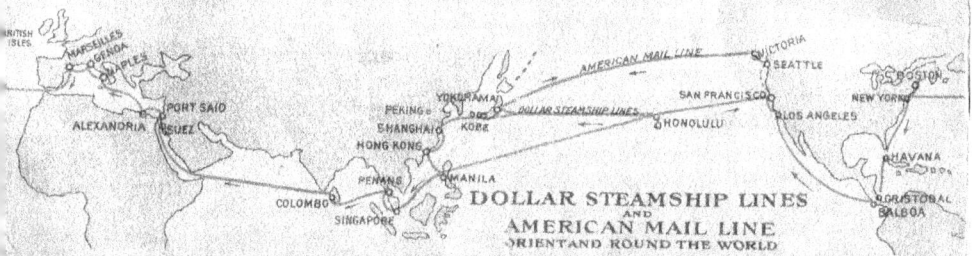

DOLLAR STEAMSHIP LINES
AND
AMERICAN MAIL LINE
ORIENT AND ROUND THE WORLD

Her [Evelyn's] diary reveals a social calendar filled with teas and tea dances, dinners, luncheons or "tiffins," bridge parties, cocktail parties and formal dances, including the annual Russian Ball.

. . . And she noted that one afternoon Mr. Chang, the head Chinese at the company, "took Jake and me to look at furs . . ." . . . A day or so later she "selected my fur coat."

W. J. Tucker

British Cigarette Co., Ltd.
Shanghai

屠
凱

大
英
煙
公
司

A VERY MERRY CHRISTMAS

AND A

BRIGHT AND HAPPY

NEW YEAR

Mr. & Mrs. W. J. Tucker, Jr.

Mr. & Mrs. W. J. Tucker, Jr.

Several remarks reveal how much her daughter's [Evelyn's] letters meant to this mother: "I had been [home] only a few minutes, when Marjorie came in with a letter from you, which meant the end of a perfect day for me." And "I enjoy your letters so much, and nothing is too insignificant to relate. . . ."

his wife out of the house t—
to us. (She doesn't speak a —
English) and then they in—
that we must go in her
room and see all the n—
cousins, children, sisters and —
children. She didn't have h—
grandchildren living there
him — eleven boys and one
was so proud of them.
That is the great aim —
Chinese wife — to bear son
husband — well there was — conflict
in that house. Ben'—' numer
children that r—   ten
years down—   there
were f—   in
the

Tientsin
Tuesday
Aug. 16, 1932

Dearest Mumsie
                    Your letter
of July 14 came yesterday
the first we had in
two weeks. Jake received
one from his mother too
and both letters mentioned
the Tuckers' visit to you s
and Aunt Gertie. Mrs.
Tucker spoke of how much
they enjoyed it and
finally "ended up" by
saying "and I fell in
love with Mrs. Harriso
Jake just as you did
that — sweet speech.
I think

My father, thirty-eight years old when I was born, had been for over ten years with the British American Tobacco Company..... the tobacco market in China was vast and lucrative. He enjoyed the work and the way of life it made possible...

[My mother] ...appreciated her role as a company wife and enjoyed traveling in society "first-class." When I was born she was twenty-nine and easily adapted to some of the customs of both British and American friends in this foreign city.

Shanghai
Sept 16th 1935.

My dear Ma,
We arrived on the 13th as per schedule after a very pleasant trip. were glad to get off the boat though as it had lasted about long enough.

We are going to be ...

Devoted Son
Fakir.

My birth certificate was a form entitled *Report of Birth: Child Born Abroad of an American Father.* Signed by the United States Consul-General, it listed pertinent data... Eventually [my parents'] copy would come to me, with instructions to guard it carefully; it was my proof of American citizenship.

REPORT OF BIRTH

CHILD BORN ABROAD OF AN AMERICAN FATHER

AMERICAN CONSULAR SERVICE

Tientsin, China, April 15, 19

(Place and date of report)

in full __Leta May Tucker__ - - - - - - - - - - - - Sex - - -fema

August 14th- - - - - - - - - - 19_34_-; Hour - - - 5:00 A

(in full) __German American Hospital, Tientsin, China__ - - -

Mother:

__William Jacob Tucker__ -

Full name __Evelyn Harrison Tuck__

Name before marriage __Evelyn Byrd H__

aucasian- - - Age -38-

Race - -Caucasian- - Age -2

Commercial business -

Nationality __American__- - -

ence __Talati House Hotel,__

Present residence __Talati House Hot__

, China - - - - -

__Tientsin, China__ - - - -

oldleaf, Virginia- - -

Birthplace __Austell, Georgia__ -

(if foreign born)

Naturalized (if foreign born)

Registered as American citizen at __Inclu in husband's registration as ox stated__

Passport No. __Included in__ xxx __husband's passport as stated__ ated

lid to

irginia, July 2, 1931- - -

Number now living - - -One-

rse __Dr. L. Brull, German-American__

ta

(Signature of parent, xxxxxxxxx)

Leta May Tucker
Aug. 14th 1934

Mr. & Mrs. William Jacob Tucker
Tientsin, China

y mail

itnesses)

(When reported in person, use this form)

in ou

Subscribed and sworn to before me this -1

-, 19

day of - - - -April- - - - , 1

at __Tientsin, China__ - - - -

Whitney Young

Consul- - - - of the United Stat

[SEAL]

of Ame

ONSULATE - GENERAL.

. . .Upon my birth [my mother] immediately hired a Chinese amah, or nanny, who had almost complete care of me. . .

Woven into my days from the beginning were things Chinese: . . . the blue satin slippers with their red flowers my amah made for me...

. . . In the spring of 1935 my father was eligible for home leave, and in April we sailed for America on the SS *President Coolidge* [where a party was held for the children].

Aunt Beck's would serve as a kind of headquarters for us while we were in Virginia and it was this part of the family that I came to know best. [Here I am with her granddaughter Betty Ran and my mother's sister, Nancy]

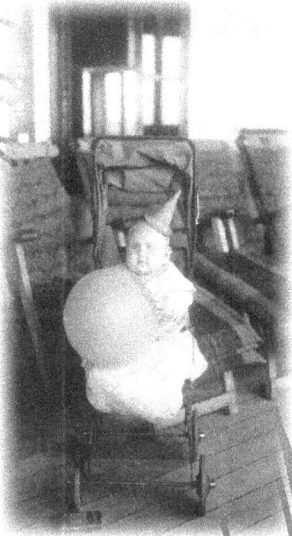

Near my birthday a large package arrived from America with a present for me from my Aunt Nancy. I was thrilled with her gift of a "real" American dress . . . I wore it along with my Chinese straw hat for my mother to take a photograph to send her.

Her name was "Lah-Nee," but to us she was simply "Amah." To her, at ages one and four years, respectively, my brother and I were—with strangers and when away from home—"Young Master" and "Young Missy."

. . . Lulu, whose special eyes opened and closed, had been a fourth birthday present. Daddy loved nicknames and he and I had a long discussion about what to name her.

. . . In Virginia we visited with family over the next four months. Photographs show a dozen or so aunts and uncles and cousins posing . . .

... It was hard for [our relatives], adults and children alike, to realize that [Bill and] I had not grown up as they had, on a Virginia farm, and that [our] China background was different even from my father's experience.

. . .These few short years at Grosvenor House were the happiest of my childhood. ...

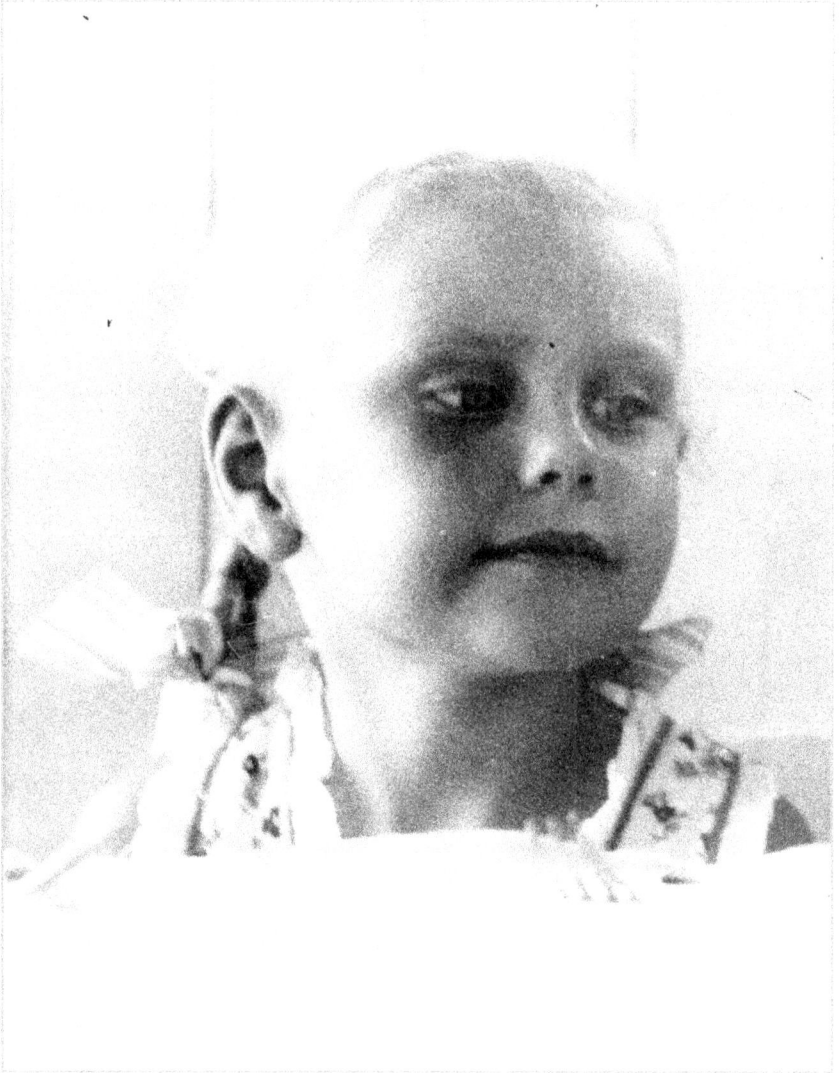

Book Two

Virginia, via Vancouver

$\mathcal{T}$he Canadian Pacific Line's *Empress of Asia*, crowded with British and American women and children evacuees, set her course from the China Sea northeast across the Pacific—away from its usual call at Japan—north toward the Aleutian Islands. From there she would veer south and east, heading for her home port of Vancouver, British Columbia, Canada.

It was November, 1940. There was no specific reason to fear any kind of attack, except that on the other side of the world Germany was blitzing England and everywhere the British Empire was in trouble. Japan, after long years of detesting the British with their superior sea power, was the newest partner in Hitler's coalition of Axis Powers and was eager to prove her worth. For decades she had limited her own hostilities mostly to the Chinese; now she was ready to further her long-planned Southeast Asia Co-Prosperity Sphere.

The United States, not yet officially involved in any war and trying to maintain her neutrality against growing difficulties, remained a giant bystander at both oceans. Her animosity toward Japan was no secret. To Americans being evacuated, witnesses to Japanese atrocities and destruction in China, Japan was despicable and unpredictable. Who knew what provocation might cause her to take action against the British—and possibly this ship, full of Americans—somewhere in the Pacific?

Wary of any unusual action on the high seas around him the captain took care to avoid Japanese or German ships and was sailing under strict blackout orders. Every night all portholes were covered with blackout curtains—and checked by ship's officers. All lights on deck were turned off and passengers were under orders not to open a door on deck or to venture out, nor to allow any vestige of light—not even a cigarette—to be seen. Aware of their vulnerability on this British ship, everyone was ready to comply.

The first two days of the voyage went as well as could be expected on this first-class luxury liner. There were so many more people aboard than normal, though, that passengers and crew alike faced difficulties. The staff did the best they could, but service was slower and the amenities of travel somewhat diminished. The crew had been unable so far to store all the trunks, heavy crates and large baggage pieces in the hold; many still lined corridors everywhere. Passengers didn't complain though, walking around them in their cabins and on their way about the ship. Despite the strain of emotional departures and crowded conditions, people were in good spirits.

My mother, suffering as usual from seasickness, remained in her bunk or in our cabin as much as possible. Occupying the adjoining suite and nearby staterooms were other BAT wives. Several were close friends, their familiar faces reassuring to me. They often checked on us, stopping in to visit and offering to watch Bill and me or take us up to the lounge.

On the third night out, however, things changed. Around two o'clock, with no warning, we were hit by a violent storm. In an instant the huge ship pitched wildly, rolling far over to one side. Everything that was not fastened down slid across cabin floors and down aisles. Heavy trunks hurtled and banged down corridors, crashing into cabin doors and blocking passageways. All lights went out. A few people fell out of their bunks. Awakened suddenly to chaos, terrified women and children began screaming. Many rushed out of their cabins into the darkened aisles; others panicked when their cabin doors were blocked. No one could see in the darkness and the first thought of many was of some kind of attack.

I awoke at the loud noise and confusion and slid as quickly as I could from my upper bunk down to my mother. Suite mates felt their way in, calling out to ask if we were okay. Within minutes a few lights came back on and the ship's officers were everywhere, spreading the word that we had run into a terrible storm but there was no cause for alarm. Constantly now the ship was heaving up and down and pitching to the side, rolling over so far that I wondered each time if it would ever come back up. I was too young to know about the *Lusitania* or the *Titanic*; others reminded themselves that a quarter of a century of maritime progress had passed since those ships met their fate.

Eventually most passengers calmed down and settled back into their bunks—if not to sleep at least to hold on to something solid. The three of us huddled in our lower bunk, very much aware of the ship's constant creaking and groaning. After a few hours, since we were already awake, my mother got us dressed and decided to go to the dining room for breakfast. We groped our way slowly in that direction, holding on to railings along the corridors and trying to anticipate each violent roll of the ship so as not to be knocked down.

It was early and only a few had ventured into the dining room. The head waiter ushered us over to the captain's table where he and another officer were seated. They greeted us and shared the latest news about the storm—probably the real reason my mother had wanted to go to the dining room. The waiter took our orders as usual.

I found it hard to eat. In the first place I had trouble staying in my chair, constantly slipping off as the ship pitched and I had nothing to hold on to. Milk sloshed out of my glass and my bowl of oatmeal kept sliding across the table out of my reach. I wasn't very hungry anyway. As was routine in a storm, the rims of the tables had been raised about three inches, keeping the dishes from sliding off. But twice I heard a load of china crashing to the floor in the galley. I wondered how we would ever eat again if all the dishes got broken.

After breakfast we made our way to the lounge nearest our cabin. This was truly a time of misery loving company. My mother—and many others—felt better if there were friends around to share the latest weather reports and discuss likely developments. They commiserated over their tough luck, but also bucked up each other's morale by staying together.

Children were particularly vulnerable to the violent rolling and heaving of the ship. One little boy named George, a first grade classmate of mine whose father was also BAT, was seriously hurt. He and his mother were in front of us as we headed for the lounge when he fell and was thrown a long way down the corridor, hitting his head against a corner and cutting a deep gash near one eye; bleeding heavily he was taken to the ship's doctor. All of us children were warned not to run and to hold on to the rail along the aisle or to anything else that was fastened down. Gradually we even became used to moving with the turbulent rising and falling of the ship, adapting, in a way, to one more new development in our lives.

The storm raged for two days and three nights, subsiding in the middle of the third night as suddenly as it had begun. The captain, apologizing later for our distress, explained that he had been unable to outrun the storm or change course to avoid it—typical of the winter weather in the north Pacific, it was large and all around us. He and other ship's officers had frequently tried to calm passengers, reporting the latest weather as far as they knew it and reassuring everyone that the storm would soon be over. After it did finally subside, the captain admitted that towards the end they had begun to worry that the ship could not hold out much longer and were pondering what action to take. It was, he said, the worst storm he had ever seen in his twenty-five years at sea.

The remaining few days of the voyage were calm and the appearance of weak sunlight did much to cheer us up. We were all glad to finally dock in the beautiful harbor at Vancouver. Though not home yet, Canada was a free, friendly land and we felt welcome.

Our stay in Vancouver was short. Along with most passengers we went immediately to the train station. Canadians, of course, headed for their homes. Americans divided, taking trains to all parts of the States. Some, mostly oil families, traveled south to California and Texas. Others—financial, utility, commercial and government people—headed across the continent to New York and the East Coast. Many of the BAT wives—the tobacco families—remained together, traveling first to Chicago and then to their home bases in Virginia, Kentucky and North Carolina.

Our route took us east out of Vancouver, across British Columbia. We rode through high, snow-covered mountains, spectacular with the sun shining on them. At Banff, a big ski resort, the train made one of its few stops. We all got out and walked beside the track for a few minutes, breathing in the cold, crystal air and marveling at the beauty around us. The next day we turned down into Montana and the Dakotas, heading for Chicago.

I loved traveling by train. As overpowering and threatening as the huge black giants seemed standing in the station, hissing steam and screeching to a stop on the tracks, trains exuded excitement and mystery. Although I disliked the acrid smell of the steam engines and the black soot that often drifted over me, I liked riding on trains. The frantic atmosphere of a depot made me uneasy, but we rarely stayed long. Everyone from conductors to porters looked out for us. It was as if we were honored guests, traveling to some special place.

Once on board there was little to do but eat and watch everything outside the window. Sometimes I played solitaire but most of the time I sat, almost mesmerized, looking out the window by my seat. During daylight if I leaned against the window and looked carefully I could sometimes see our train, made up of a dozen or more cars, curving around a mountain so that our engines were silhouetted against the sky. Steam streaked back over the cars. Sometimes we crossed from one mountain to another over deep canyons on sky-high, skinny bridges—it felt like we were riding on air. Later we passed through small towns and I could watch people on the streets and sometimes see farmers in the fields.

At night a strong beam of light cut the blackness in front and we seemed all alone in the world. In our stateroom I slept in the upper bunk and could look outside at the lights in the villages we passed or see the headlights of cars stopped at the tracks. The engineer often blew our whistle, high and piercing, and we went shrieking our way through the darkness.

We didn't stop much. Before dinner in the evening a kitchen car was hooked up to ride for a few hours at the rear of our train, or food supplies were transferred from another train over to ours. At the depots we saw only a few people, mostly railroad workers. It must have been very cold, for they were all bundled up and hurried to do their jobs. Often these workers, seeing children at the train windows, would wave to us and we always waved back, happy to be noticed.

I especially enjoyed meal times—once I got to the dining car. I dreaded going back and forth from our stateroom or the lounge at the rear of our car to the dining car. The doors separating the cars were extremely heavy and hard to handle; I was afraid I would get caught in one. My mother picked up Bill and held my hand, but even she had difficulty. The platform between cars was almost out in the open and not only was it bitterly cold, but the noise was excruciating and the wind so strong I felt I might be blown off.

Inside the dining car, as soon as the door closed behind us, everything was calm and serene. Spotless starched white cloths covered the two rows of tables. The places were set with heavy pewterware, big linen napkins, sparkling glasses of ice water and thick chinaware bearing the emblem of our train line. The menu was large and impressive. My mother would give our order to the black waiter, who usually laughed and joked with Bill and me. I liked the food, but was never very hungry. At each table, next to the window was a small lamp with a shade; it was fascinating to look out and see the other diners reflected in the window beside us.

Finally we reached Chicago. This time we would not visit anyone but merely change trains for Richmond. This meant a lot of moving of luggage and the necessity of picking up tickets, arranged by the Company and waiting for us.

My mother settled Bill and me and all our baggage on one of the benches in the enormous, high-ceilinged station and then went over to the ticket counter. For some reason she was directed to another counter at the other end of the station. I watched her walk away, her high heels clicking on the hard floor, and then lost her in the mob of people milling around. Suddenly I was terrified. What if she didn't come back? I didn't know the name of the town we were going to, and I didn't know the last name of Aunt Beck or Nancy or anyone else. How would they find us? Finally I made out my mother far down at the other end of the station. In a few minutes she turned and headed back across the waiting room to us.

A red cap loaded our luggage on his cart and we followed him down to the correct track and boarded the train for Richmond. As soon as we were settled I made sure I knew the name of the Virginia town where we were going and the last names of Mama's family.

We pulled into Richmond's Broad Street Station late the next evening. Here we had to change stations as well as trains so my mother had decided to spend the night in the nearby William Byrd Hotel. It was a Sunday night and the dining room was closed, but they sent sandwiches up to our room. Then Bill began to act up, crying for Milk of Magnesia. Over and over my mother calmly explained that we didn't have any and he didn't need any. Then he threw a real tantrum. At her wit's end, she called the head desk and asked if they could get a bottle for us, which they did. Bill was given a good dose, and exhausted, he finally fell asleep.

The next day we took a taxi across Richmond to the Main Street Station and after a short wait boarded a local Seaboard Airline train for La Crosse. Some of my mother's family were waiting at the station.

At last the long, difficult journey was over. Even though it had been barely a year since we had left Aunt Beck's, everything once again seemed strange. I was stiff and anxious and so very tired as we walked back into her house. But I was grateful to be there. It was, after all, the closest thing we had to home and these wonderful people were, whatever might happen, our family.

Getting Settled

$\mathcal{T}$he first few weeks after we reached Virginia were filled with the bustle and excitement of an American Christmas. In the front hall at Aunt Beck's a mound of brightly wrapped presents dwarfed her tree. In the kitchen pantry sugar cured ham, chess pies, chocolate, pineapple and coconut cakes sat on their special shelf, looking and smelling delicious. Holiday thoughts helped bring a smile to my face and ease the tension that had been with me for so long.

On Christmas Eve I walked with Aunt Beck and Betty Ran to the Methodist Church for their Sunday School party. We listened to the Christmas story, received our gifts of hard candy and an orange, and sang carols. My favorite was "There's a Song in the Air." On our walk home I kept thinking of the words about God. *Hadn't I always known that there had to be Someone like that?*

On Christmas morning amidst great excitement we all opened our gifts. Then we sat down at the dining room table, set with the family's best china and silver, for dinner. For dessert we had ambrosia, something made only once a year at Christmas, along with cake. It was a special time for my mother's family, almost all of whom, beginning that afternoon, came to see us. Her Grandma Bowen, now age ninety-six, we had already visited.

With the calm and cold of January, however, reality set in and my mother was faced with many decisions. Only a few letters got through from my father, and he had little to say that helped her. He, too, had no idea how long he would be in Shanghai or when we might be able to return. Not knowing what might develop, she was trying to decide where we should live. We were welcome at Aunt Beck's, but she felt three more people crowded them too much. She finally decided to look for an apartment in Richmond, where a number of BAT wives were living.

In the meantime we spent several days in Petersburg with China friends who had just moved into a new house. I still remember the snow, the beautiful winter sunsets, the lack of furniture and the make-shift beds, since their heavy household boxes had not yet reached America. There were no children here, and Bill and I, though we tried to behave, were not very happy.

We then went to Washington, D.C., to stay for two weeks with Grandma Tucker, Aunt Rosa, Aunt Bertha and Uncle Don and their children, Peggy and Joyce. It was really a full house. They all welcomed us and were very kind to us. They, too, were worried about my father. My grandmother in particular kept saying that she wished "Jake would come on home before something happens."

I was always uneasy when we were visiting somewhere, and will never forget how Joyce, two years older, looked out for me. She was in third grade at one of Washington's large elementary schools, and on several days when she walked back in the afternoon after coming home for lunch, I was sent back to school with her. I sat scrunched up next to her in her desk, very quiet, and listened to all that went on. The bigger boys teased us when we walked home, but Joyce would protectively put her arm around my shoulder and tell them to leave us alone. I was always so glad to get back to her house.

By the first of February we had moved to Richmond, a block or so from Uncle Holmes, my mother's brother. Our two-bedroom apartment, on the second floor of a typical brick city house, was rented furnished, with two beds, a sofa, kitchenware and little else. Bill and I slept in one bedroom, he in a borrowed crib that he was too big for, and my mother across the hall in the other bedroom. I remember trying to roller skate on the front sidewalk and walking to the grocery store a block away. I also remember having terrible nightmares in which huge growling dogs chased me. I would wake up terrified, but not wanting to bother my mother, would get my bearings by the street light shining in the window, and eventually go back to sleep.

Despite the doses of cod liver oil and orange juice administered daily by my mother, Bill and I had suffered from one cold and sore throat after another ever since we had reached Virginia. After another round of illness Mama was advised by the doctor to have our tonsils removed, a routine operation for many children at that time. Grandma Tucker came down from Washington to be with her as we underwent tonsillectomies at a nearby hospital. We stayed for three days and fared well, recovering with the help of much vanilla ice cream and strawberry jello.

My mother was not happy living in Richmond. She had no car, no help with Bill and me, all the cooking and daily chores to do, was uneasy alone in the apartment—and very lonely. After only three months she decided to give up the apartment and go back to

La Crosse where she knew more people and would be near more family. Bill and I were delighted to be going back to "Grandma's." We were now calling Aunt Beck "Grandma," since Betty Ran called her that and it seemed the easiest thing for us to say. The fact that she and Uncle Jim, now "Grandaddy," accepted this new status and treated us as such, brought an added semblance of stability into our lives for which I was forever grateful.

In June, after school was out and Nancy could join us, we spent several weeks at a small boarding hotel at Virginia Beach. This proved to be a good vacation for all of us. Then we went to Roanoke and stayed two weeks with Nancy at her boarding house.

By the first of August, with little favorable news coming from my father and the international situation worsening, my mother took a room in La Crosse at Mrs. Thomasson's boarding house. Our room was small and crowded, with a bathroom down the hall shared with other boarders—quite different from the lavender and black marble bath of home. There was, of course, no amah to help with the laundry, getting me dressed or making my bed. I didn't much like the food, but I knew this was no time for fussing. I had to "make do," I was told, with what we had and be thankful.

I found it hard to understand the money situation. Money, it seemed, "did not go as far" as in China, and my mother seemed hesitant about any spending. In China, while not "wealthy," we were, especially in comparison to thousands of destitute Chinese, certainly well off. In America, particularly in this post-Depression small Virginia town, we were far from it. My mother sewed dresses for me from seed sacks—as did most other mothers. When I went to school I felt lucky to have two dresses that I wore on alternate days to school and one nice, "store-bought" dress for Sunday. Among my classmates one boy, a distant cousin whose father was in the wholesale candy business, and I were obviously better off than the rest. But no one was "rich."

One of our fellow boarders was a young woman named Lillian who became a lifelong friend of my mother's and a special favorite of mine. She owned and operated a small beauty parlor, the only one in town, and had many customers. Her husband soon went into the Army and she was as lonely as we were. She not only washed my hair, carefully braiding my two plaits, but let me come and visit after school. She also gave me my first job—washing and drying the shop's combs and brushes. The extent of my duties was limited, but my pay was a nickel a week and I felt very important.

Things improved when my mother bought a car. After much discussion within the family and much worrying about whether she could afford such a big cash outlay, she decided on a slightly used '39 two-door black Chevrolet. This gave us all a sense of freedom. I didn't always have to walk the long hill over to Grandma's— sometimes we could ride. My mother felt better and now was able to leave us at Grandma's while she drove to Richmond and Roanoke for extended visits. She was especially glad to have contact with other BAT wives and to compare notes about what they heard from their husbands and what was happening in Shanghai.

Despite the crowded and difficult conditions at Mrs. Thomasson's, I was glad to stop moving around. In September of 1941 I entered second grade and with that daily routine established I felt we had finally gotten settled.

Second Grade

$\mathcal{E}$very eye in the small crowded schoolroom I had just entered turned to watch as I walked over to the teacher's desk. My mother had taken me to the principal's office to register as a new pupil, but now I was on my own. On my own among these two dozen curious second-graders, not one of whom I knew, but every one of whom knew me as "that girl from China." The fact that I was blond, blue-eyed and spoke with a British accent confused some and convinced others that I was not at all what I was supposed to be. Nevertheless, despite the differences, I was now one of them.

Since I had not completed grade one—I had not attended school since I left the American school in Shanghai the previous fall—there was some question about my entering grade two. We had moved around too much for me to start back to school, so my mother had helped me learn my letters and numbers, and I could read a little. The second grade teacher, Miss Hattie, was a former schoolmate of my mother's, so the two discussed my situation at length. Finally she agreed to enroll me in the second grade. If I

149

couldn't handle it after a few weeks, I would be put back into the first.

So I began second grade, uneasy with so many strangers, unfamiliar with the school routine and more or less on probation. I knew I could not fail or dire consequences in the form of deep disappointment on the part of my mother would result. My strong desire to succeed and my God-given quick mind carried me through those first difficult weeks.

The La Crosse School, grades one through eleven, was an old brick building on the edge of that small town. My mother had gone to school here and here my grandmother had taught seventh grade. Most of the teachers were old friends of my mother's and several remembered my grandmother. With the exception of my cousin, Betty Ran, and a few of her friends—all sophisticated fifth graders—I knew no one. But I wanted very much to "belong" and to be like the other children and while uneasy, was glad to finally be going to school.

The small cramped second grade classroom boasted a blackboard across the front, racks and shelves around two walls and two big windows on one side, as well as an outside door. Five rows of small desks, heavily varnished, each row with five seats, faced the blackboard. The desks, made of wood and well worn, were bolted to the floor, the flat top of each attached to the fold-up bench in front of it; under the desktop was a space for books. Everything was crowded and it was hard to move around the room. Sweaters and caps hung on pegs at the back, tin lunch boxes and paper lunch bags lined a shelf, and around the walls hung a big portrait of George Washington and a few other bright pictures. Across the top of the blackboard in beautiful handwriting—what my mother would call "Locker"—stretched the letters of the alphabet. I felt a stab of concern about this, for I had never practiced printing letters and certainly did not know handwriting. I was assigned a seat in the middle of the room and someone helped me hang up my sweater. It was very warm and with twenty or so pupils crammed in the room, the air was stuffy.

Our daily routine began, as it would every morning, with Miss Hattie reading the week's Bible verse, also written on the board. After that everyone stood and recited the Lord's Prayer, which I knew from Sunday School. Then came the Pledge of Allegiance to the Flag, a ritual completely new to me. I watched carefully, turning to face the flag hanging over the blackboard and placing my hand over my heart as the others did, but at this point I faltered.

Not only did I not know the words, but for some reason that I did not understand the effect of the flag upon me was so powerful that for weeks every time I looked at it I had to fight back tears. Nothing else had brought home to me how precious this country was, how much I missed my father, still so far away, how relieved I was to be safe in America. I felt confused and bewildered. I wondered if anyone would understand if I tried to explain and somehow I knew they wouldn't. I tried to concentrate on the words they were all saying. Then we sang the first verse of "America" and finally, shaking inside, I sat down. Although I quickly learned the words to the Pledge, it would be a long time before this routine would become comfortable for me.

I never talked about home—about Shanghai. No one, not even the teacher ever asked me about living there and I never said anything, knowing that no one really was interested. It was as if I closed a door on that part of my life—except for Daddy.

I soon discovered that I could read well enough, if not better than most. Our reader was a *Dick and Jane* book and easy. It was one of several textbooks we were to study, and at this school we purchased our own. When I took the book list home, my mother quickly approved my buying new ones. I loved the smell of the new books and the touch of the smooth, shiny new pages. There was not only the green and black reader, but also a thin orange speller with its lists of words, some of which I already knew, and a big thick arithmetic book. I made a special trip to the grocery store with Betty to buy a "Red Chief" lined tablet and two yellow pencils with erasers. I loved the way a trimmed pencil cut so neatly into the soft paper—so sharp and precise; an eraser messed things up so I tried never to have to use it. The lines of sums blocked across a page looked so efficient and I was so much in command of the answers—how I relished the red "100" mark at the top of my first arithmetic assignment.

Though at first I dreaded recess, I soon became friends with two other girls sitting near me. Nancy had brown pigtails like my blond ones and Pauline was small with bright red hair. Sometimes we sat outdoors on the two stone steps leading into our classroom and talked and ate our lunch, sometimes we climbed up the old wooden "grandstand" or bleachers by the dirt ball diamond, and sometimes we played in an area near our class door, a piece of bare, sandy ground under a clump of tall pine trees. With pine needles and sticks, and sometimes bricks if we could find any, we each outlined our own house, with several rooms, floors of sand, front and back "doors" and a piece of wood to sit on. We spent much time marking off rooms and sweeping the dirt floor with bunches of pine needles. Then we went visiting. Nancy and Pauline, despite many a spat between them, both stuck with me and gradually I began to feel accepted as well by the rest of the class.

After Christmas the chickenpox descended upon us one by one

and in late winter, after suffering with several colds, I came down with it. I had to stay in bed, quarantined, for the better part of two weeks. Betty or a friend brought me my school assignments so I would not fall behind, and I carefully did all of them, not wanting to chance being "put back." Fortunately I had mastered the classwork so well by this time that I felt fairly sure that I could stay in second grade. I spent the rest of the time listening to the radio and reading.

I owned only two or three books and they were too "young" to be interesting. There was no library in town or at school, and no store selling books. Whenever my mother went to Richmond she brought back a book for me. The first was a Bobbsey Twin book, which was okay, but my favorite was a Nancy Drew, *The Mystery of the Missing Map*, followed by *The Mystery of the Moss Covered Mansion*. I was fascinated with them and read them over and over. Gradually I was able to get others, and for years I continued to enjoy those books as well as the children's classics received at my birthday and at Christmas. Given a choice I always asked for a new book. Other favorites included *Pollyanna*, *Magic for Marigold*, *Elsie Dinsmore*, *The Littlest Rebel*, *Anne of Green Gables* and later, *Little Women*.

Another event of that second grade year, though exciting, was sad and unfortunate for all of us children and for both school and town. On a windy night in April most of the school building burned to the ground. Fire fighters couldn't save it. I was spending the night at Grandma's since Mama was away on a visit. Betty and I were surprised that morning when no one called us to get up. We straggled downstairs only to be told the news. Betty immediately wanted to go and see what had happened. Grandma wavered about whether I should go, but finally agreed. I set out with Betty to join other kids walking over to the school. We weren't allowed to get very near for it was still smoking. Almost all of the old building had been destroyed. Outside our second grade room I could still see the two stone steps, but everything else was gone.

The worst thing to happen during this year, however, concerned not school but my father, the war and the nation. On December 7, 1941, the Japanese attacked Pearl Harbor.

Along with most other Americans I well remember that Sunday afternoon. We were at Grandma's house and had just finished Sunday dinner. Betty and I were playing paper dolls, Grandaddy was taking his nap, and the other grownups sat around talking. My mother, as she often did, turned the small radio on for the two o'clock news.

Suddenly she turned the radio louder as special news began to come in—confused and garbled reports that were so horrible that at first no one would believe them. I listened to all they were saying and knew that something terrible had happened. In those few minutes America changed. Within days the United States would be at war with Germany, Italy and, of course, Japan. For the next four years all of us would be acutely aware of the war.

My mother's first thoughts, reflected in the strained expression on her face and in her words, were of my father and what this might mean for him and for all Americans stranded in China and the Far East. She did not say what this also might mean for the three of us.

My own thoughts were a scared, confused muddle. I knew what war was. Exactly where was my father? And what would the Japs do to him?

Winter Rainbow

We were many months without hearing a word from my father. We had been apart for a year at the time of Pearl Harbor; it would be another two years before he would come back to the States. I was six years old and in first grade when we left him, nine and in fourth grade when I next saw him.

Earlier in 1941, in a letter sent with a friend traveling home by boat, my father summed up the Shanghai situation: ". . .Things are about the same here as they have been for the past year or so. A bomb or two every day or so with a few hand grenades mixed in. Also a murder nearly every day, not to mention kidnapping, robbery, etc. Most of this among the Chinese. . ." Only a few letters coming by regular mail—and air mail service was nonexistent— had reached us in Virginia. After Pearl Harbor all correspondence stopped. Occasionally my mother received a letter from the BAT stating that my father, as far as they knew, was well.

Thinking that his family would want to know something of his life during "these trying times," he began a sketchy journal. The first pages record what he did on Monday, December 8, 1941— December 7 in the States:

> On the morning of Dec. 8 I was awakened at three a.m. by a terrific explosion. As sounds of this sort are not unusual in Shanghai and have not been unusual for the past 4 years, I did not think a great deal about it and went back to sleep.
>
> At five-thirty a.m. our senior Chinese, Mr. William Wei, telephoned me that the Japanese had blown up the U.S. ship "Wake" as well as the British ship "Petrel," [in the Whangpoo harbor] and that all bridges leading to Hongkew were closed. I reported to Mr. Grant and we decided that we would attempt to go to work as usual. . .
>
> I went to the [Garden] Bridge at 6:30 a.m. The information regarding the bridges was correct as they were all closed and occupied by Japanese troops. Quite a few of our foreign staff were waiting there, as well as a large number of Chinese.
>
> While discussing the situation. . . heard that the Japanese flag was flying from the mast head of the "Wake" . . .[I replied that] I would have to see it before believing it to be true. With three or four people in the car with me, I instructed my chauffeur to drive along the Bund. . . .We had just passed the Custom's Inspection shed when the sound of rifle or machine gun fire was heard from the river and the enormous crowds of Chinese there on the Bund scattered in every direction. A Japanese cruiser was lying along side [the shed] and in the cold grey morning light we could see sailors dashing around the decks either cleaning the guns or loading. . . The "Wake" was not in sight and as we realized that it might be extremely

dangerous to go any further we decided to return to the Palace Hotel.

We were all very much excited and after discussing the situation over the telephone with Grant we decided to return to our homes. . .

A few minutes after returning home. . . a close personal friend of mine who was connected with the U.S. Consulate here, called me and stated in a very official tone of voice that a state of war existed between the United States of America and Japan. All Americans were advised to stay indoors and not to go on the streets except in cases of emergency.

Things were quiet in the French Concession. Japanese soldiers paraded on the Bund and moved about the main streets of the International Settlement. He spent most of the day at the apartment, often on the phone with company officials. That afternoon he joined a few friends at the nearby French Club. With no reliable news reports it was difficult to piece together what had happened. For a while the events at Pearl Harbor and the Philippines were not fully grasped, but there was no doubt that the U.S. and Japan were now at war.

The next day the company's assigned Japanese "contact man" directed BAT officials to open their factories as usual on December 10 under the control of the Japanese Navy. This met with confusion, he wrote, as it was difficult to operate factories when considered prisoners of war, but with the company's directive and some misgivings he went down to the Thorburn Roads plant and got it into operation again. It soon became clear that Japanese officials were going to stay on the premises and after gradually taking over all papers, documents, etc., would take control of the factory.

They quickly posted a large "Proclamation" warning of severe consequences to anyone breaking their rules.

Though my father remained nominally in charge, he had to obey their instructions, even to having large groups of Japanese appear time after time for elaborate tiffins and detailed inspections. He also had to join them in photographs taken of "the staff." The BAT management instructed him to cooperate in every way and to give any information or documents asked for; they had decided that this was the only way to avoid arrest or other unpleasant consequences of disobeying their captors—in particular, being imprisoned in the infamous Bridge House. With their knowledge of Japanese jails and methods of treating prisoners, none dared to deliberately cross them.

As Japanese took over more and more control of the factory his salary was cut, far below what was needed to maintain his usual life style. Another BAT colleague and friend joined him in our apartment; sharing expenses for food helped them both. By summer he was only going to the factory one or two days a week. The Japs had taken over the entire operation but still demanded his presence on various occasions.

Other changes began to appear in the immediate aftermath of the Japanese takeover of the city. Private automobiles were not allowed on the streets without special licenses. Since Daddy's factory was six miles away, this meant riding a Chinese bus or tram—something he had never done before—to Hongkew and then transferring to a Japanese bus. It was an unpleasant and time-consuming experience, made worse by the crowds of Chinese coolies of the lowest class now taunting all Westerners at losing their former ruling position. Under special circumstances he was permitted to use the car and chauffeur but was then subject to search by Japanese marines. On one such trip from the factory back home he was stopped twice and searched, but allowed to pass.

Life continued as close to normal as possible. The price of food went sky-high but was still plentiful if you could pay. Meat cost $10 to $14 (Chinese money) a pound, one chicken, $46. With the approach of Christmas everyone thought that since their country and the rest of the world were at war they would have a miserable holiday, he wrote, "although we realized that we had and still have a lot to be thankful for. . . . But at the last minute people began calling each other up and asking them to Christmas Dinner just as if we were not prisoners. . ." He and the house boy had gotten together "four turkeys, a couple of hams, and a few other things of that kind given to me by our Chinese dealers" so he invited sixteen guests for tiffin. "They appeared to have a good time," he noted, "and seemed to forget for a while the fact that all of us would give anything in the world to be with our families."

As the months dragged by my father recorded several sad developments within the Western community. An American friend with whom he had played golf when they were both stationed in North China committed suicide. When one BAT man, a Canadian, died suddenly of a heart attack he commented on how much he would be missed and on the shock and difficulties in notifying his family, then in Canada. And one evening at Grosvenor House there was the sound of sirens and many cars entering the compound. When he looked out the dining room window he could tell from the black cars and their flags that these were high Japanese officials. They pulled up and stopped at the main entrance. Then, as he watched, from the apartment just above him, where an American businessman lived, he heard the distinct sound of a pistol shot. Rumored to be an American spy, this man had chosen that path, he commented, rather than "go with our friends. . ."

In May of '42 he was able to send a few lines home through the International Red Cross. It was brief: "I am well. Trust you and children are same, advise Mother. Love you, Tuckey and Bill. Jake." At Christmas of '42 came another similar message and that was all. My mother also sent Red Cross messages, never sure that he would receive them.

In July he noted that "War news is not good." It was also scarce and inaccurate. Shanghai newspapers were publishing only under Japanese control, if at all. They reported, he wrote, that the allied fleets had been destroyed "several times" and that the war "was practically over." Added my father, "the Japs are taking over everything in this part of the world." Short wave radio from San Francisco supplied some facts which circulated among the Americans and British but during the early, desperate months of 1942 even that fell silent.

By the fall of 1942 Japanese control tightened. Red arm bands with an A for Americans and a B for British were issued to all British and American subjects. They were warned not to go outside their own houses without it worn on the left arm. Once he forgot his and had to go back home to get it. "Enemy subjects" were forbidden to attend movies, theaters, prize fights, bars, dance halls or eating places where there was music or any other entertainment. Strict black outs were held at night. Eventually there would be complete house arrest for all "Enemy Nationals."

By November the Japanese began rounding up people for their civilian concentration camps. The first group to go, to Haiphong, numbered around four hundred, including sixty Americans. Some were his "close acquaintances" and one a friend and distant cousin. Rumors spread that they would all be interned within a week. These proved false, but most Americans packed two suitcases and were ready to go at any time.

In January one hundred Americans and three hundred Britishers—all men—were interned at Pootung, across the Whangpoo in the BAT's "No. 1 Factory." In February another large group was taken, including a number of BAT executives and several close friends. On the first of March he was still out, but on the 12th, along with approximately a hundred others, Daddy was sent to Pootung.

For weeks in late 1942 and early '43 he had waited, under house arrest, to be ordered into camp. One thing he did as soon as this seemed likely was to burn all papers, letters, etc., knowing that nothing of a personal nature could be kept in camp. Among them was an old invitation from General Douglas McArthur and another from D. D. Eisenhower to play golf on military facilities in the Philippines—a certain danger if the Japs saw them. All letters from my mother and his family he burned, and even the small Bible his mother had given him, because it had a personal inscription inside and therefore would be taken.

He debated what to do with the large framed color photograph of Mama, Bill and me that sat on the living room mantle. Finally he walked across the foyer to the opposite apartment where a Swiss family lived. They spoke German and he did not know them but they were Swiss and therefore immune from Japanese control. He asked the lady of the family if she would be so kind as to keep the picture for him until he returned. She graciously nodded, and as he handed it to her, in broken English she promised to take care of it, smiled and wished him well.

He now had his two suitcases, one crammed with all the canned goods he could carry, packed and ready. His journal, a small, lined ledger, he put in with his clothes, hoping it would escape inspection. At the last minute he picked up a small red cigarette box with an ivory figure on the front, one of his earliest purchases as a bachelor in China, and stuck it in.

At the appointed time he and one colleague, among the few BAT men still out, met outside Grosvenor House as instructed, boarded a Japanese Army truck and headed for the river. Chinese servants solemnly watched and then left. Apartment 303 now stood empty.

My father never spoke of some of the things he had written in his journal. Parts of it reveal something of his state of mind. After his description of the morning of Pearl Harbor, December 8, 1941 comes this section:

. . .As we left the Hotel we saw a very unusual sight: a rainbow at 7:15 a.m. on a winter's morning. As we stood in the doorway of the Palace the rainbow was directly over the Whiteaway Laidlow Building. I have no recollection of ever seeing such a sight on a winter's morning.

Amid the uncertainty, danger and anxiety of that day he apparently found some comfort in the age-old promise of the rainbow. Perhaps he thought of it again as he faced the ordeal he knew lay before him at the Pootung Civil Assembly Camp.

Pootung Camp

On March 12, 1943 my father entered the Pootung Civil Assembly Camp as a civilian detainee of the Japanese Army. Much of the information about his time there comes not only from his journal but also from the stories he told on those rare occasions when he, and perhaps a friend or two, talked about "camp."

Located in Pootung, across the Whangpoo harbor from the Bund, the Pootung Camp was one of several civilian concentration camps maintained by the Japs in and around Shanghai from the fall of 1942 until the end of the war in August, 1945. None of these camps was on a par with the infamous "Bridge House" in downtown Shanghai, where political prisoners, suspected spies, prominent citizens and such were incarcerated; those inmates were badly tortured, beaten, starved and otherwise mistreated, many who entered never surviving to leave. The civilian camps were intended for the civilian citizens of those countries at war with Japan. Nevertheless, individuals lived in constant fear that any trifling occurrence might prompt punishment or their banishment, for no known reason, to the Bridge House.

The Pootung Camp, one of the first to open, was located in a confiscated BAT factory compound. Several of the three- and four-story brick factory buildings were now serving as quarters for over a thousand British, Dutch and American internees, including the crew of the *U.S.S. Harrison*, captured in the harbor at the beginning of the war. While other prisons also housed women and children, all in this camp were men. Among the Americans, forty states were represented. Except for the navy men almost all were over the age of thirty-five. Many were executives, managers and businessmen associated with the banks, trading firms, oil and tobacco companies of Shanghai. Some, both American and British, were employees of the BAT, men like my father who had managed or worked at this factory in past years and were familiar with the buildings and the area.

My father was assigned to Section 24, Room A16 on the third floor, a small area near a corner window. Among the sixty-six inmates on this floor were a number of BAT men whom he knew well. Three who had been there several weeks and were already settled into the camp routine, welcomed him on his arrival, having prepared his cot and "space" for him. They included him in their four-man mess group—one cooked, one set the table, one washed dishes and one dried. Daddy became the dishwasher.

Food, at least for the early weeks of his stay, consisted mainly of fish, with a little meat twice a week, and rice. This was supplemented by any canned goods they might have brought with them or any food they could afford to buy from the camp's "canteen," such as eggs and bacon. By early summer the camp stopped the fish and internees were given buffalo, goat and occasionally a little pork. The rice became poorer in quality, often infected with dirt, bugs, worms and such. As the months passed the supplies in the canteen, as well as their supply of money to buy anything, also dropped lower and lower.

The inmates of this "Happy Home," as the Japanese insisted on calling their camp, were allowed a few small plots of land for gardens. Some of these tobacco men grew up on farms and knew how to raise a good crop of vegetables as well as tobacco. Working in groups, they planted lettuce, onions, tomatoes and carrots. Before summer, however, these gardens, near the outside boundary of the camp, were "fenced out" by the Japs. Even smaller gardens were then planted inside a closer fence. The plot Daddy's group worked was dubbed "Tobacco Road" and its bounty added substantially to their meals.

One day each week, upon request, two of their gardening group were allowed access for an hour in late afternoon to their first vegetable plot. One of the men, Mr. Savage, a BAT executive and close friend of Daddy's, would always go to collect any available vegetables. On that day, at that time in the afternoon, his former Chinese house boy would appear and walk slowly past the outer compound, just beyond the fence—never speaking, never making eye contact, but merely walking past. He never once failed to come. It was a show of loyalty that did much to raise the morale of his former employer as well as some of the other men who had known him.

One of my father's favorite stories about his time in camp concerned his visit to the dentist. He lost the filling in a tooth and was suffering with a bad toothache. His request to see a dentist went through the channels and one morning he and three Britishers were allowed to go across the river to a Japanese dentist. One Japanese guard accompanied them in a launch. They got safely to the dentist's office and settled down in the waiting room. Their bedraggled guard also took a seat, looking like he needed treatment himself; he soon dropped off to sleep, snoring loudly. Daddy and the other three in turn each went in to see the dentist, who spoke no English. And the guard slept on. When the four were finished and the guard still slept, Daddy rather strongly said that *he* was certainly not going to wake up their guard, derelict as he was in his duty. So they all sat and waited. It grew later and later, until at last one of the Britishers tapped the guard on the shoulder and said they were ready to go. Embarrassed and disgruntled, the guard got up and led them back out to the street and down to the launch. Nothing was said about the guard's long nap. By now it was raining and when they reached camp around six o'clock they were soaked. Daddy's messmates came through for him with hot coffee—the real thing, carefully hoarded—and a better than usual dinner. He, in turn, reported on his day's activity—and an opportunity not taken.

Not all of the guards were so grouchy and one had a real sense of humor. No radios, either long or short wave, were allowed in camp. All had been confiscated and violation was a serious offence. One short-wave set, however, had not been turned in. Keeping it well hidden, its owner every few days brought it out briefly for news of the war. While this was going on everyone on the floor was on the alert for any Japanese guard. If one should appear, someone was to yell out the old British hunting call, "Tallyho!" This would be repeated and passed from section to section throughout the floor. The owner would then immediately stash the radio away in its hiding place. Guards approaching the third floor became accustomed to hearing the call of "Tallyho!"

Then came the morning when one guard arrived on the third

floor and no one noticed him. To the astonishment of inmates throughout the floor there suddenly rang out the familiar "Tallyho!"—but with a decided Japanese accent. The guard, well aware of what was going on, had a good laugh. Inmates had a few tense moments, but the radio remained undiscovered.

A diary entry sums up the daily camp routine:

> *June 16th, 1943: A beautiful summer morning. Far too beautiful to be locked up for nothing and with nothing to do except eat, wash dishes, make up a bed—and mop the floor. All of which is finished by nine fifteen. Very hot yesterday and will be the same today. . .*

The inmates passed much of the time by playing poker, bridge, mah jong, dominoes, cribbage, Black Jack and other games— most with a bet on the side to make it more interesting. Credit was freely extended. There was even a P.A.W. (Pay after the War) poker game, the largest game in camp. Eventually, though, even the games began to pall. Their few books were read, passed around and re-read. One BAT friend had bought or traded for an accordion and set about teaching himself to play, providing a topic of some complaint after exceptionally long sessions of practice, but he did learn some pieces.

They also were allowed to play baseball. The navy men had enough equipment and they marked off a field in a section of the dirt compound. One big game featured the crew of the *Harrison* versus the BAT. The sailors were younger, but the tobacco team won out, 5-1.

On August 11 my father marked the twentieth anniversary of his arrival in China. There was little celebrating, however, as the tail end of a typhoon hit Shanghai and a terrific wind and heavy rain continued all day. Late in the afternoon a portion of the roof on their building was torn off and it looked like the whole roof might go. Until noon the next day they had no electricity and no water except what was pumped up from the river. Rain blew into their room through the windows as well as the roof. It was a "dreary time," he commented, but a few played poker by the light of a candle stuck in the mouth of a bottle. The wind destroyed the laundry, a shed with an iron roof, the Japanese guard house and a portion of the garden.

A few days later he wrote: "The garden has been closed since the storm for no reason except downright meanness. People with laundry were allowed out to do some washing yesterday and a few were allowed twenty minutes to get vegetables from the various plots in the outer garden. J. G. brought in a nice lot of tomatoes. Tobacco Road came through the storm well. . ."

Two journal entries close out the story of his stay at camp. On August 16, 1943 he wrote:

A lot of things have happened since the last entry. About July 15th a letter was received from the Japanese Consulate saying that a second repatriation ship would leave Shanghai about Sept. 1st, maybe earlier, maybe later. About July 20th a letter was received from the Swiss Consulate outlining a new classification of Americans and Dutch. Married men who sent their families home are now according to this list in a better position than bachelors and others. We are now in Class 5 which should give us a good chance of getting away on the first boat if and when it goes.

And on August 21 the last journal entry:

> *Lot of excitement in camp yesterday. A member of the International Red Cross visited the camp. While here he stated that the* Gripsholm *has left New York for Goa carrying supplies for the RC in the Far East. Lots of conflicting rumours as to whether it is bringing Japs and will carry some of us home. Only time will tell who is right.*

As it turned out Daddy's name was on the list of those Americans slated for the *Gripsholm* exchange. On a hot day in early September of 1943 he packed all he could in a pillow case, hid his journal, hoping he would not be searched, and he and the other repatriates, as instructed, prepared to leave camp. A launch would take them to the *Teia Maru*, anchored in the Whangpoo harbor. This Japanese ship, once it collected those repatriates listed for the exchange in Shanghai, would call at other Asian ports—particularly Manila, where a large number waited to board—on her way to Portuguese Goa, near India, where the *Gripsholm* was to dock.

The next hour or so my father once called among the worst of his life. It was extremely painful for him to leave many of these close friends and fellow inmates. With some of them he held bonds of friendship reaching back twenty years. With others there were more recent ties but strong attachments due to their common experience in camp. They had all stuck together for many months; he almost felt that he could not leave. Who knew, war being war, what the outcome of their stay would be.

The entire camp assembled outside to say goodby. And the entire camp fell silent. Without speaking, the remaining internees formed a long double line out to the camp fence. As the men to be exchanged walked, single file, down the aisle, past their fellow inmates, toward the outer gate of the prison compound, all of those remaining stood at attention and saluted.

So my father and the other repatriates walked in silence out of the Pootung Civil Assembly Camp, down to the Whangpoo wharf and aboard the waiting launch. Far, far ahead lay home.

Waiting, Ever Waiting

$\mathcal{I}$n the meantime, back in La Crosse, Mama, Bill and I waited. Waited, along with the rest of America, for the end of the war. Waited for my father to come to the States. Waited for us to move out of temporary boarding places into our own home. Waited for our lives to return to normal.

When I finished second grade, and after visiting here and there over the summer, we left Mrs. Thomasson's and moved into the La Crosse Hotel. This plain, unpretentious structure had been built around the turn of the century to accommodate railroad personnel as well as visitors to town. A two-story, long brick building, it had faded over the years and grown grimy with train soot and cinders. Railroad tracks were only a short distance beyond the yard and gravel road that fronted the hotel. It now presented a bedraggled appearance to visitors as well as those living there.

We had two adjoining bedrooms on the second floor. From the ceiling of each room hung an electric cord with one light bulb and switch. My narrow, single bed was made of iron pipes; white paint flaked off the headboard. At bedtime I stood on the end of my bed, turned the hanging light switch off and then crawled under the sheets. There was a small sink with running water in one room, while the bathroom was down the hall. The whole set-up was crowded and dingy looking. Even the straight, coarse lace curtains at the windows were no longer white but tinged with gray. On one wall we tacked up huge maps of Europe and the Pacific and carefully followed the progress of the war. These were not colorful, cheerful rooms. I did not, however, dare complain.

Mrs. Willis, the present owner, was a widow who managed the hotel with little help. Being a large woman and often in the kitchen, she had a reddish complexion and always looked to me like she was about to burst into flames. Everyone thought her an excellent cook. Her fried chicken was exceptionally delicious and appeared frequently, as did her canned peaches. For me, her culinary blue ribbon went to her chocolate cake—six layers of "yellow cake" with chocolate frosting measuring at least a quarter inch thick between each layer and on top. To our delight one appeared almost every week.

While we lived here I entered third grade and in the fall of 1943, the fourth. With no piano, after school I would walk up to my mother's friend Miss Katie's house, find the hidden front door key, let myself in and practice for an hour in her living room. During school months it was always so cold I kept my heavy winter coat on. The room, sparsely furnished, unused and musty, seemed eerie at times, especially since no one else was in the house. But at least I kept up with my piano lessons.

I could walk to Grandma's without crossing the railroad tracks, so I went whenever Mama would let me. Sometimes I was asked to stay for a meal—this was particularly welcome on Saturdays at noon, when the hotel's menu consisted mostly of navy beans. On Sunday night Grandma often invited us for supper since the hotel dining room was closed. She often served oyster soup with tiny round crackers, and pie or cake left over from another meal. Anything we ate there was always delicious to us.

My mother constantly worried about trains. The town's two railroad lines were a commanding presence. The Southern, on the edge of town, was not so much for passengers as for produce, and there were fewer trains running. The Seaboard divided the town in two and to get to the Post Office, drug store and other stores on the main street we had to cross the double tracks. Our ears became acutely tuned to the long whistle of an approaching train, but it was many months before we were allowed to cross by ourselves.

The trains of the Seaboard Airline were long and on a crowded war time schedule. At night they seemed to thunder straight through my bedroom. I often woke up around two o'clock when the *Orange Blossom Special* passed through on her way to Florida, and a half hour or so later when the *Silver Meteor* came shrieking through on her way north. They normally did not stop at this small town except for a serviceman. The screaming whistle reminded me of our train rides and now I felt doubly safe in my bed. Eventually I would go back to sleep.

In the spring of 1943 my mother received word from the BAT that Daddy was well but was interned in a Japanese civilian concentration camp in Pootung. Other than that we knew nothing. I began to forget what he looked like, but I did have a tiny silver locket with a small snapshot of him and I wore the locket every day. Some of my classmates were now telling me that they knew my father was not in China at all, but really was a convict in the penitentiary. I learned to pay no attention to them.

My mother heard through the BAT and finally through the U.S. State Department of a possible exchange of prisoners—Japanese officials in return for Americans such as my father. The *Gripsholm*, a neutral Swedish ship, had already made one such trip, and another exchange was expected. For months delay followed delay. Correspondence with the State Department included letters to and from officials regarding my father's status and whether or not he would be eligible to be exchanged on the next ship. For months we were not sure whether it would sail again, and if it did, whether he would be on board.

By fall of 1943 newspapers reported that the *Teia Maru*, the Japanese exchange ship, had sailed for Goa, near India, where it would meet the *Gripsholm*. It had already stopped at Shanghai to pick up those repatriates. Not until word came from the State Department listing Daddy's name did we really believe that he was on it. After boarding the *Gripsholm*, the repatriates made the long trip around Africa and across the Atlantic to Rio de Janeiro and then continued up to New York City, landing in early December. My mother was waiting for him at a New York hotel where they stayed a few days before catching the train for La Crosse.

Bill and I were staying at Grandma's during this week. We were allowed to miss school the day Mama and Daddy were expected back. I wore my new rose-colored pleated wool skirt and blue sweater for this very special occasion and Agnes helped me with my hair. I was so excited that for days my stomach hurt and I couldn't eat much.

As excited and grateful as we all were at my father's safe return this marked the beginning of a difficult period of adjustment for each of us. It was not easy for Bill and me to get used to his presence after three years apart. There were problems between my parents, not helped by our crowded living conditions. We visited family everywhere, interrupting my school work and upsetting all routine.

By spring Daddy was assigned by the BAT to a position with an associated tobacco company in Richmond. We rented a furnished house on Stuart Avenue—a two-story brick house with large rooms, ugly furniture and creaky old floors that I came to hate. I enrolled in fifth grade and Bill in first at the William Fox Elementary School, a walk of several blocks from our house. In class I faced a clique of girls not easy to get to know. My teacher, Mrs. Rodden, carried me through with her kindness and efforts to encourage friendship among all of us. The next year when I left I regretted having to leave and I think some of them were sorry to see me go.

During that fifth grade year, in April, President Roosevelt died. We were dismissed early from school to go straight home. When we turned on the radio it played only classical music; the entire nation mourned. My classmates and I had never known any other president and wondered how the country would manage.

Not long after, it was announced that the war in Europe was over, though fighting in the Pacific continued. But the tide had turned and the news reports were filled with names such as Iwo Jima and Okinawa. In August came rumors of a terrible new "atomic" bomb and then we learned the names of Hiroshima and Nagasaki.

On August 14, my eleventh birthday, came word that Japan was ready to surrender. That evening we piled into our car and Daddy drove down Broad Street past throngs of people, all shouting, hugging each other, laughing and brimming over with joy. Church bells rang, cow bells clanged and automobile horns blared, as did sirens and blasts from factories. For some, tears flowed. Excitement and relief filled everyone. At long last, the war was over.

The next three weeks were filled with phone calls, telegrams and letters from the BAT, friends and business associates of Daddy's. They were eager to get back to Shanghai to claim their own property as well as that of the company, and to save what they could of the BAT factories. Soon he was notified that arrangements were being made to fly some of the men from California to China by military planes; his name was one of the first on the list.

Mama, Bill and I also had to make immediate plans for our future. Women and children would not be allowed to return to China yet; once again we would be on our own, without Daddy. Our big question was whether to stay in Richmond. We couldn't remain in the house where we were and decent housing was expensive and very scarce. Finally we decided to return to La Crosse to stay at the Hotel, in the same old rooms plus one additional bedroom.

I entered sixth grade. I was back among familiar faces again, but the school work was not nearly as challenging or as interesting. The only bright spot was the nearness to Grandma, Betty and the rest of the family.

Always we seemed to be waiting for word from Daddy. Letters could now be sent by airmail, though the schedule was haphazard and costly. Most came by way of people flying to the States, carrying letters to be mailed to us upon their arrival. We heard very little but knew he arrived safely, was back at the same factory compound and was living in our old apartment at Grosvenor House.

In late spring of 1946 the BAT announced that they—and the U.S. State Department—were ready to allow women and children to return to Shanghai. Daddy submitted our names to the company. By early June came word that we were booked on the *SS Marchen Maersk*, a Danish vessel, due to sail at the end of July. The waiting was over and the time for action had come again.

On the last Saturday night at the hotel I listened, as usual, to the radio program "Your Hit Parade," with its rundown of the songs popular during the previous week. At the end came their theme song: "So long for a while, that's all the songs for a while. . ."

The tears were near as I lay in the hot, humid darkness and felt again the pain of leaving a familiar place. I had mixed feelings as I thought about the long trip back and what lay ahead. I kept reminding myself that I was really—wasn't I?—just going back home.

The Journey Back

Hey, Bob-a-re-Bob. . . Hey, Bob-a-re-Bob. . . The deep, black, velvety bass voice of a longshoreman rumbled up from the lower deck to the small stuffy cabin where I sat.

Hey, Bob-a-re-Bob. . .

A second worker echoed the words and then a third, farther down in the hold, repeating the popular song then playing on America's radios and juke boxes. Keeping the rhythm, they unloaded hogsheads of tobacco on to the deck and rolled them down into the ship's hold. Over and over they sang the song, keeping the beat and stacking tobacco, the bulk of the cargo on board.

It was July 30, 1946, less than a year since the end of the war in the Pacific. We were on board the *S.S. Marchen Maersk*, a small Danish freighter out of Copenhagen, Denmark, in port at Newport News, Virginia. After a lapse of six years we were starting the long trip back to join my father in Shanghai. He had gotten word of our plans and a cable awaited us when we boarded ship:

*Mrs. Tucker Passenger Marchen Maersk, Newport-News Vir
Wonderful news relax aboard ship Tuckey & Bill will look
after you, Love Jake*

This was the best ship the BAT could find for our journey back
to China. No splendid luxury liner was available, as most of them
had seen heavy service in the war and were being repaired and
renovated. This small freighter, too, had been a troop ship, carrying
men and supplies back and forth across the Atlantic. Now ready
for peacetime commerce, it carried extensive cargo and twelve
passengers. We were three of the twelve.

We had been assured that the entire ship had been cleaned,
fumigated, painted and decked out with new furnishings for this, its
first postwar voyage. But on this still, hot, humid day I sat huddled
on one bunk in a cabin that reeked of mildew. Everything smelled
strongly, overwhelmingly and unmistakably of mildew. Upon
questioning, the purser insisted that the mattresses, pillows and bed
linens were all brand new but had been sitting in a warehouse where
they got damp and mildewed. The smell permeated the cabin. There
was no use complaining; all we could do was get used to it. Going
out on deck in this busy, noisy harbor would not improve things
and there was no place on board that offered any respite from the
heat. We were hot, uneasy, uncomfortable, unhappy—and at least
two of us were suffering from severe homesickness.

We were supposed to have sailed the previous afternoon. Several
of the La Crosse family had driven down to see us off only to hear
that our departure had been postponed until the next evening.
They had gone home, leaving us despondent and disheartened. If
we had sailed as scheduled, without such a long wait and lack of
movement, we might have avoided such feelings of despair. But the

delay had been long enough to allow my mother, always a hesitant traveler, second and third thoughts about the looks of this ship and the long voyage that lay ahead of us. After a miserably hot and smelly night in the small stateroom she broached her fears to us at breakfast the next morning.

"Maybe we shouldn't go on this ship," she said. "Maybe we should just go back to La Crosse and take another ship later."

I said little. It was Bill, with his eight-year-old confidence and curiosity, who brought us back to reality.

"But we're already here and ready to go." he said. "We can't get off now!"

I could almost see my mother squelch her "nerves" at Bill's encouragement. After more discussion we decided to stay on for the five days to Panama and the seven days up the west coast to California. If we couldn't bear it any longer, and the trip across the ocean seemed too much, we would get off there and take the train back to Virginia.

It was a badly needed escape hatch. Bill appeared to be satisfied and my mother's frame of mind lifted a little. There was a way out of this after all, I thought, and I, too, began to feel better.

As the afternoon wore on, the sky grew dark, clouds warned of a coming storm and a strong breeze began to blow. We were due to sail around six and shortly before, with no fanfare, we moved from Newport News into the Chesapeake Bay and the Atlantic Ocean.

The next day proved far from calm as we passed Cape Hatteras. The wind was cold, the sky overcast and the dark gray sea "heaving mightily" at the effects of the storm. Bill and I managed to stay up for a few hours, but my mother was quite ill. In my diary is the note: "I wish I were any place but on this boat. I am so seasick."

By the next morning, with a clear blue sky above, a deep blue ocean beneath and a bright sun shining, the ship leveled off and we all felt better. While the seas continued rough for the next two days, we managed to get out on deck and soon developed a normal routine.

It had not taken Bill long to explore the passenger area of the ship and to learn his way around. The ship had eight staterooms, on two decks. There were two cabins on each side of a small dining room on the lower deck, and two on each side of a large, open lounge, backed by a row of windows, on the middle deck. We had one cabin on the lower level and one directly above it on the lounge level. Above that were the captain's quarters and the upper deck.

We had met the other passengers before we sailed. My mother was especially pleased to see Mrs. Mae Folts, whose husband was with Standard Oil, whom she knew slightly. She and her thirteen-year old son Franklin would be going the full distance with us. He and Bill immediately became friends and allies.

By far the most intriguing of the few passengers was Mr. Lederer. Probably in his sixties, his baggy clothes hung loosely on his thin, stooped frame, he had a deep scar over one eye, walked with a marked limp and spoke English with a heavy German accent. He seemed to be everywhere, listening to every conversation. It took us only a few days to decide that everything about him shouted "German spy!" In this postwar era of German retribution, we were positive that he was a Nazi escaping authorities and heading for Shanghai, the place he claimed was home. How fair an assessment this was we never learned, but for the entire trip, for one reason or another, he remained a mystery.

We also became acquainted with the ship's personnel. The captain, a round little man with a fair complexion and a bushy red mustache, was in his sixties, friendly and outgoing, though he spoke little English. As far as I could tell he spent most of his time in his upper deck cabin, where he enjoyed a splendid view, ate meals off trays and indulged in his hobby of oil painting. Sometimes he was at the steering wheel, surrounded by all kinds of instruments, and sometimes he relinquished the wheel to the first mate. Bill and I were invited in to visit several times. I especially admired the dozens of lovely paintings lining his large circular cabin. Bright and colorful, many depicted the sea and its changing moods, others probably his home in Denmark. Once, later in the trip, we were each allowed to take a turn at the steering wheel.

The purser disappeared once we were at sea. Appearing to take better to alcohol than to sea water, he made himself scarce and departed the ship in California. No one seemed to miss him and no one took his place.

The most important of the crew to us kids were Fak and Peter. These two young men, barely twenty years old, served as dining room waiters, cleaning stewards and general persons you called when you needed something. Fak had dark hair and eyes and was very conscientious. Peter was blond, very good looking and always concerned with some deep personal crisis. On the lap from Panama to California, he fell madly in love with one of the passengers, the daughter of a wealthy businessman on board. When she fell just as hard for him, he became rather lax in his duties. Rumor had it that he wanted to "jump ship" in California and get married, but her father's disapproval and the Captain's threat of "dumping him from the crew" and seriously damaging his future prospects, apparently had their effects. Once she disembarked at California Peter shaped up, more or less, for the rest of the trip.

Fak was really our friend. He spent an inordinate amount of time keeping Bill and Franklin out of the dining room, where they often headed, hoping to filch a few sugar cubes from sugar bowls kept on the tables. When the war shortages eased back at home, we had grown used to an occasional candy bar, cookie, Coke or Pepsi. Now we had nothing. The ship had loaded up with crates of soft drinks but they were some unknown brand that none of us could stand to drink. Nor did the ship, taking on more supplies in port, take on board any more desirable items. Sugar cubes were not Hershey's chocolate but they did assuage a sweet tooth—and besides it usually brought Fak out of the kitchen to talk to us.

The dining room, or mess hall, was small. One table stood in the center, seating six or eight, and three smaller round tables in the corners, each seating four. Most of the time we had a corner table for just us three.

On the sixth day out we reached Panama. The ship docked at Christobel, letting off several passengers, and prepared to go through the Panama Canal, then United States territory. We waited in line for the official paper work to be done and then the ship began to progress through the locks taking us from the Atlantic over to the Pacific. In some stretches the canal itself was so narrow that you could reach out and almost touch trees and vegetation growing along the banks. I tried to remember details about the locks from my geography book but simple observation was better and explanations by the American pilot on board gave us an excellent understanding of how everything worked. Although very hot, we enjoyed the all day diversion of the canal and the beautiful scenery. At the other end we took on more passengers and sailed into the Pacific.

Sailing up the coast to California turned out to be perfection in a sea voyage. The sea looked as smooth as glass. With no waves or white caps, the water appeared to be a huge, unwrinkled sheet of beautiful blue silk. A slight breeze kept us just cool enough and we spent hours out on deck.

Among the new passengers was Peter's big crush, sixteen and very pretty. She and her father dominated the scene. The father, a big strapping man with a deep, booming voice, was almost as mysterious as Mr. Lederer. In fact we wondered if he was living some kind of dual life. He dealt in fine jewelry—diamonds, gold, jewels, and handmade necklaces, pins and bracelets—but he also talked constantly—and loudly—about connections and jobs with the Panama government. On this trip he was taking his daughter to the States to enter college. Somehow he found out that my birthday was coming up and he presented me with a special present, a lovely little gold filigree pot of gold hanging from a small bar pin. I was delighted with it and often wore it.

On the fourteenth day of the voyage, in mid-afternoon, we docked near Los Angeles at San Pedro. Mrs. Folts and my mother were eagerly anticipating some good American food and a chance to shop for some last minute items in Long Beach. Despite the expected high cost, they called a taxi. Because of the great distance involved—we were more than five miles away from the main part of town—and the poor condition of all taxis, we were asked to share the one large cab with anyone else going that way. We agreed and when it arrived the five of us piled in along with two of the ship's crew.

One, the first mate, had stashed a huge piece of machinery into the trunk of the taxi. He quickly volunteered that it was the ship's steering apparatus—something was wrong with it. He and his shipmate giggled and settled in the front seat.

"Ach," he said in his broken English. "Very bad! Loose and goes crooked." With that his hand made a swerving path across the back of the front seat and he and his crew mate laughed heartily.

"But," he said, "we fix! Tonight!" And the two laughed again. "No worry!"

At this Mrs. Folts and my mother visibly paled. In fact we all looked askance at the two crewmen. We were not sailors, but we did understand the necessity of proper steering.

The cab driver finally arrived at a main shopping area and stopped for us to get out—the steering wheel and crew members were going on to some shop. The street was crammed with sailors on leave and the two mothers, growing more and more apprehensive, warned us kids to stay close to them. Mumbling something about having landed "in the middle of the red light district," they led us quickly into one of California's new super drug stores just up the street.

We wound up at a sandwich counter for dinner and then did our shopping all in the same store. Gathering up movie magazines, crossword puzzles, baseball cards, playing cards, Hershey bars and Life Savers, Bill and I soon spent our allotted funds and were begging for even more items to assuage the anticipated boredom of our shipboard life. Eventually, as it was getting late, our mothers called a stop. But finding a taxi driver willing to take us on the long drive back to the docks proved a real problem. Several declined the job, saying their broken down pre-war vehicles and worn out tires wouldn't make it that far. Finally one agreed to go, charging, said my mother, "an arm and a leg."

The next day, August 14, marked my twelfth birthday. Before we left La Crosse I had received my main birthday present, a ladies wristwatch, yellow gold with a black corded band. I had been asking for one for months and wore this, my first watch, with special pride. I didn't expect much in the way of more gifts or celebration, but I certainly didn't look forward to spending a long, hot, boring day aboard ship.

Mrs. Folts had called friends living in the area and she and Franklin planned to spend most of the day with them. The ship wasn't sailing until six o'clock, so my mother decided to splurge on another taxi ride to one of the swanky hotels in Long Beach. We had a delicious birthday lunch at the Hilton Hotel and then walked around the shops and grounds. Bill was sent into a barber shop to get a haircut—at the "exorbitant" price of one dollar—and we caught another taxi back to the ship with time to spare. Nothing more had been said about our leaving the ship and heading back east; we were ready to brave whatever storm—or lack of steering—lay before us.

By six that afternoon six new passengers had boarded, word had spread that the ship's first mate had returned with a repaired steering wheel and all was set for our departure.

We pulled away from the pier into choppy waters and a cloudy sunset. As I stood on deck and looked back toward shore the last thing I saw, clearly visible in a strong ray of sunlight, waving in the strong breeze, was an American flag.

Slow Boat to China

 $\mathcal{J}$ ak was sounding the bell for dinner as the coast of California faded into the horizon behind us. As I turned to go down to the dining room, I was thinking that once more my birthday had brought something unusual. I knew it would be a long time before I again laid eyes on America.

The six new passengers who boarded at San Pedro were gathered in the dining room and my mother and I paused to meet them. Two were middle-aged missionary ladies returning to the interior of China. They appeared at a few meals and occasionally on deck in the evening but otherwise had little to do with us.

Another new passenger was assigned temporarily to our table, a Mr. Mandrell. He was a California dealer in expensive *haute couture* ladies' shoes and handbags. A world traveler, he was now on his way to meet his fiancee in Calcutta, where they were to be married. He implied that she was Indian, but we were never sure. I always thought him somewhat evasive and even insincere in his conversation but he was a charming talker and a welcome new face at the table.

Our dinner that night was fancier than usual in order to welcome the new passengers. This ship would certainly not be remembered for its mouth-watering cuisine; it was solid cooking, more in the British tradition. Desserts were either fruit such as my favorite mangoes or puddings of dubious nature. Tonight, however, we were in for a surprise.

After our table was cleared for dessert, I looked up to see Fak carrying in a large tray that he placed with a flourish in front of me. On it, with twelve small lighted candles, sat a large birthday cake—a large, pale green birthday cake. I looked at it in astonishment.

The other passengers—even Mr. Lederer!—lifted their water glasses in a toast and sang "Happy Birthday." The head cook leaned out of the kitchen door to see my reaction and others on the kitchen staff peered out of the other door's round window. Fak and Peter were both grinning and stood ready to help me cut the servings and deliver them to the other diners. I made a wish, blew out all the candles and cut the first square piece.

It was the saddest looking cake I had ever seen. The outside was a mottled, streaked chartreuse and the inside a pale yellow. The icing, thick in spots, in other places had dribbled off the cake onto the tray. Barely legible were white letters saying "Happy Birthday."

It was also the worst cake I ever tasted. The yellow part seemed to lack some major ingredient or else something had been substituted. The green icing needed sugar or a sweetener and had a peculiar seasoning in it. It was Mrs. Folts who later said she thought the cook had used one of the cake mixes new on the market but had somehow made a mistake in the ingredients or didn't have something essential for both the cake and the icing—like sugar. Honored by such a gift from cook and staff, I didn't care and ate every crumb on my plate.

When we left the table I went back to the kitchen to thank the staff and suggested that Fak and Peter, the cook and all the kitchen help should each have a piece. They all smiled and clapped. I remained delighted, despite the cake's odd taste, at such a wonderful birthday celebration.

The other new passengers included a lady and her ten-year old son Mike. A tall brunette in her early thirties, she was stunningly beautiful. Both Mrs. Folts and my mother knew of her as the wife of a wealthy American wheeler-dealer/businessman/trader in Shanghai, but neither knew her personally. She retreated to their cabin on the opposite side of the ship and we saw nothing of her for the rest of the trip. Mike became a welcome fourth to us kids, but he seemed apprehensive, very concerned about his mother and sometimes limited in the amount of time he was allowed to spend with us.

The remaining newcomer was a retired businessman. He soon made it known that he was taking this trip as a relaxation cruise because of a severe heart condition. His cabin was one of the four opening to the lounge—we had one, Mr. Lederer one and Mr. Mandrell the other. Always worried about the lack of a doctor or any medical expertise on board, Mrs. Folts and my mother were particularly concerned about Mr. Hadley. He was overweight, red in the face, short of breath and "didn't look good."

The five of us, old hands by this time, had slipped into a daily shipboard routine. We ate breakfast around eight in the dining room and then went out on deck, sometimes to walk around, sometimes just to sit and watch the ocean. Later in the morning, as it grew hotter, we wandered up to the lounge. The adults discussed any late bits of shipboard talk and wondered what was going on in the outside world; we were totally removed from any source of current news.

We kids usually settled down at one of the two new lounge booths with their padded leather seating, to play cards. We began with "Old

Maid" and then moved on to our favorite, "Hearts." This usually kept us occupied until lunchtime.

Lunch, served in the dining room, generally consisted of omelets. We had omelets of every kind and description. Certainly the cook was not hampered by a shortage of eggs on board, eggs that we strongly suspected were of the dried variety. Occasionally sandwiches of bologna, salami or very oily, thin peanut butter on "home baked" bread appeared, with fruit for dessert.

After lunch the adults retired to their cabins for a long nap. Sometimes I did, too, reading my movie magazines and books over for the third and fourth times, but often I joined the boys in the lounge. There we continued our card games, or played ping pong, now fast losing its charm, or watched Franklin do magic tricks.

Bored and hot, with nothing interesting to do, our afternoon sessions often wound up with singing. There were few songs that we all knew, so we soon moved to Franklin's favorite, the only one we all could sing. We began quietly: *"Ninety-nine bottles of beer on the wall, Ninety-nine bottles of beer. . ."*

Not once, but twice, and even three times we would go through the whole rigmarole, getting louder and louder. We knew that eventually Mrs. Folts or my mother would come out and demand that we stop lest among other dire possibilities we cause Mr. Hadley, in the stateroom next to us, to have a heart attack. So, worn out anyway, we would stop. For that day.

It was my mother and Mrs. Folts who almost had heart attacks one miserably hot afternoon. Leaning out of the lounge window, Franklin casually announced that the crew had just gotten out several hoses and were watering the dozens of barrels sitting on the deck below us. These had been loaded on ship in California and crowded around our '39 Chevrolet, anchored in the middle of the deck under a canvas

190

cover. Furthermore, added Franklin, he thought that the reason they were doing this was because across each barrel was written the word "EXPLOSIVES."

This brought both mothers to their feet. Mine recalled seeing something on the boarding agreement indicating this. They quickly got their tickets and there, plainly written across several pages, in red ink, was the large word "EXPLOSIVES." The tickets went on to state that the chemicals in the shipment were those otherwise known as dynamite.

After the initial excitement things calmed down, but every day from then on hoses trickled cool sea water over dozens of barrels of dynamite on the deck below us. Both mothers resigned themselves to the inevitable, adding to their list of dire possibilities, explosion at sea.

It was only a day or so later that Franklin, lacking anything better to do and in a mischievous mood, began to strike the few matches remaining in a match box he had found. He would watch the flame burn out, and then casually drop the extinguished match out the window—down on the lower deck, on top of the dynamite barrels. When his mother came up and saw this she lost her usual calm composure, her lovely complexion turned red and she lit into Franklin. He received a severe tongue-lashing and a punishment that stopped him in his tracks. It had a big effect, too, on Bill and Mike.

In the meantime we were all having trouble with water of another kind. The plumbing, starting in Mrs. Folts's bathroom, which backed on ours, got more and more sluggish and finally stopped working entirely—in all the cabins. There was no water. We promptly informed Peter and Fak, who informed "the plumber," who responded valiantly to the call. After things were temporarily repaired we were told to ration water, meaning that the frail showers and any baths were out of the question.

The plumber, if this was an accurate sobriquet for him, was a sight to behold. A large man, he was always clad only in shorts and undershirt, both of which were streaked with black grease, as were his shoes, his arms and legs, head and face. He was apt to appear at any time of day or night. We would hear a timid knock at the door and open it to find him standing there, grinning. "Hullo," he would say—the only word of English he knew—and wait for us to usher him into the bathroom. At this point I usually fled to the lounge, but Bill and Franklin eagerly observed him at work and even got him to take them with him down to the boiler room. This was probably his natural habitat and how he acquired the accumulating layers of grease that covered him from head to heavy shoe.

As willing as he seemed to be in regard to fixing the plumbing, and as genial as he was in arriving at our staterooms to get to work, he never, in spite of long hours of trying, got the bathrooms on our side of the ship permanently fixed. They would work for a day or two and then the call would go out again for the plumber. The best he could do was appear, giving us the illusion that help had arrived. We finally realized that he knew very little about plumbing, and in the absence of anyone who did, had simply been named the designated plumber. We became rather attached to him, though, knowing that he would at least appear and somehow get a little water flowing again.

Despite the monotony of the journey there was one part of each day that was, for me, pure pleasure. After dinner in the evening I would always go up to the small upper deck to watch the sunset. Sailing west, we were always facing a magnificent setting sun. Brilliant colors—rose and russet and red, orange and magenta, deep gold, pale yellow, delicate pink and lavender—filled the entire sky and were reflected in the ocean. Every evening I soaked up the sight of the sky and the sea; I felt like I was storing up this splendor for the rest of my life. Later, when the sky faded and darkness fell, I sometimes stood at a lower deck's railing and looked at the "diamonds" down in the dark water. Here you could see tiny streaks of light—phosphorescent flashes in the sea. There was always something spectacular to look at. We even spent several days watching for a whale that a crew member thought he had spotted.

We were near the International Date Line, where we lost a day, August 23, when we noticed a trail of churning water behind us in a wide zigzag pattern. The ship, instead of sailing in a straight line was making wide turns and leaving a wake of "Zs." When it continued for several hours, we sought answers of Peter and Fak. They asked the crew, who said the steering system was acting up again and they were working to correct it. They thoughtfully sent word that soon "all be okay."

At about this time, too, we began to catch whiffs of strong ammonia. This continued for several hours. We wondered what was going on but were assured that nothing was amiss. There was little we could do anyway but trust the captain and crew for whatever might go wrong.

We were about a week from port, nearing several Japanese islands, including Okinawa, when we noticed another pattern of zigzagging and a slowing down of the ship. We were barely crawling through the water. The captain explained that this part of the ocean had been mined during the war. Several of the crew were ordered on deck to keep a sharp lookout for mines, and the first and second mates were told to steer a slow zigzag course in order to avoid them. This appeared to be the accepted approach to getting through the treacherous waters of this part of the Pacific.

The lookout for mines certainly did not ease our minds, it being a rather immediate "dire possibility," but by this time we were immune to worry. We all were resigned to whatever fate might lie in wait for us. At last, when we spotted the hazy outline on the distant horizon that was Kyushu, Japan, we knew we were getting close to the China Sea and journey's end.

By the first of September we began to anticipate our approach to the shores of China. A cablegram to the ship also confirmed that we were relatively close to the China coast. It was addressed "Note to Leta Tucker" and simply said "Happy Birthday # Dady." One of the crew delivered it to me on a tray from the kitchen. It wasn't much, but it did lift our spirits and assured us that the end was almost in sight.

After a day of sitting in the steaming China Sea, we moved ahead into the Yangtze Basin and eventually up to Woosung. It was here that my father arrived by launch to join us and we boarded a river tender up the Whangpoo. The Shanghai harbor marked the end of our long, long voyage.

I viewed the skyline of the Bund as it lay before me across the Whangpoo with a sense of adventure and excitement—and a feeling of anxiety. Had this place always filled me with an undercurrent of dread? What a long road I had traveled since I last had seen it. For a while I had thought I would never return. But here we were again, whether I liked it or not. It was, for better or worse, Shanghai once more.

. . . Not packed were the wooden junk that sat on our living room
mantle; a large framed, tinted photograph of Mama, Bill and me...

Most Americans in Shanghai planned for departure as soon as possible.

At last the long, difficult journey was over. . . . With the calm and cold of January, however, reality set in and my mother was faced with many decisions.

. . . We were now calling Aunt Beck "Grandma," . . . The fact that she and Uncle Jim, now "Grandaddy," accepted this new status and treated us as such, brought an added semblance of stability into our lives for which I was forever grateful.

Returns From The Orient

Mrs. W. J. Tucker, above, whose husband is connected with the British-American Tobacco comany in Shanghai, returned to the United States with her two children in November on advice of the state department and their passports are being held up until conditions become more settled in China. She is visiting her sister, Miss Nancy Harrison, 604 Allison avenue, S. W. (Times Staff Photo).

Shanghai Not As Pleasant As It Once Was, Visitor Says

Mrs. W. J. Tucker, Separated By War From Husband, Hopes To Return

Conditions in the Orient are being watched with a prayer by Mrs. W. J. Tucker, now visiting her sister in Roanoke, so that she and her two children soon may be able to return to Shanghai where her husband is connected with the British-American Tobacco company.

She and her two children, six-year-old Leta May, and William Jacob, Jr., just three, returned to the United States in November on advice of the state department and their passports are being held up until conditions become more settled in China.

In September of 1941 I entered second grade and with that daily routine established I felt we had finally gotten settled.

Earlier in 1941, in a letter sent with a friend traveling home by boat, my father summed up the Shanghai situation: "...Things are about the same here as they have been..."

Only a few letters coming by regular mail...had reached us in Virginia. After Pearl Harbor all correspondence stopped.

Shanghai
July 10th 1941

My dear Ma.

How I enjoyed your letters. Hope you are much — it is too hot here to write or do anything much. The world war spreads from place to place but old Shanghai carries on just the same. With the exception of high prices in rent food & etc. conditions are about as usual. A few people are murdered most every day but that has been going on for years.

I am glad you are down at Willbos with Evelyn. I hoped she would stay there for a month or two more but it is up to her to do what she thinks best.

Hope Albert is better now. The Suckus & Tennis are sure multiplying rapidly. They sure are all well. Hope I'm home as if we might get home sooner as usual four years but definite this time with —— for this time with all your —— —— Jake

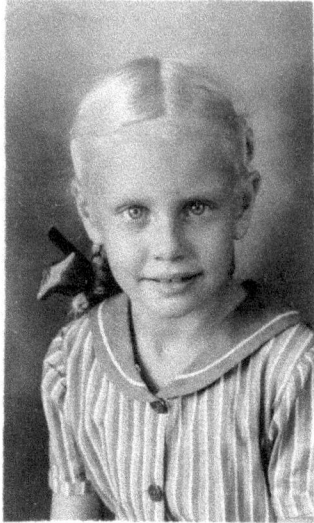

. . . sent to America, along with some of our household goods, were the Chinese treasures my parents had collected over the years: . . . two carved teakwood cedar chests; two Chinese rugs; a prized tea set; the bamboo china set; dozens of linen tablecloths; two old Chinese tapestries; small inlaid tables; ivory figurines. . .

His journal, a small, lined ledger, he put in with his clothes, hoping it would escape inspection. At the last minute he picked up a small red cigarette box with an ivory figure on the front, one of his earliest purchases as a bachelor in China, and stuck it in.

On the first of March he was still out, but on the 12th, along with approximately a hundred others, he was sent to Pootung.

. . . I did have a tiny silver locket with a small snapshot of him and I wore the locket every day.

— but at the last minute I managed to get away.

It is beautiful in the garden today lots of children playing and older people taking sun baths. I still cannot go out there without thinking of our kids & and the good times we had playing together. I miss my family so much it is a bitter pill to be away from them but so many people have suffered so much more that I realize that we still have a lot to be thankful for.

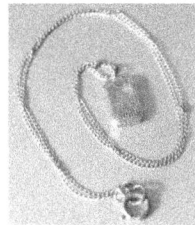

By fall of 1943 newspapers reported that the *Teia Maru*, the Japanese exchange ship, had sailed for Goa, near India, where it would meet the *Gripsholm*.

RIGHT
THUMB
PRINT

William J. Tucker
Signature of Bearer

Repatriates Await Transfer To Gripsholm

By PRESTON GROVER

MORMUGAO, Portuguese India (AP)—The American consulate announced today that the exchange of American and Japanese nationals aboard the liners Teia Maru and Gripsholm will take place tomorrow beginning at 8 a. m. (11 p. m. Eastern War Time today).

The announcement was made by the consulate after a conference with Japanese authorities while the expectant repatriates hung over the rails of the two vessels eagerly awaiting their transfer.

It was ____ed that the Japa____ ____ day's delay in the ____le them to finish ____ accommodating

____is, it was a one-____ of the holiday ____ting 21 months ____ aboard the Gripsholm to enjoy the cheeses, meats and swe____ have been the ____ during ____

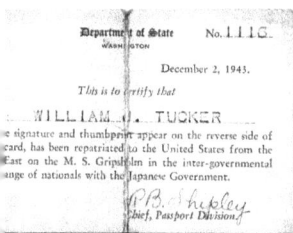

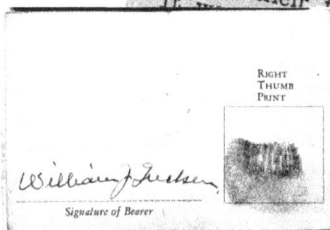

EXCHANGE SHIP ARRIVES AT INDIAN PORT—The Japanese exchange ship, Teia Maru, arrives

. . . After boarding the *Gripsholm*, the repatriates made the long trip around Africa and across the Atlantic to Rio de Janeiro and then continued up to New York City, landing in early December.

Repatriates Exchanged at Indian Port

By PRESTON GROVER

MORMUGAO, Portuguese India (AP)—Like holiday picnickers but with much deeper joy, 1,500 Americans and nationals from other countries in the western world today marched off the Japanese ship Teia Maru and boarded the exchange liner Gripsholm which will carry them home after months of internment in Japanese hands.

Again free men, they stepped into the hot sunlight shouting jokes and wisecracks.

A file of stony-faced Japanese, being exchanged for the Americans, ten yards away contrasted with them as they marched off the Gripsholm.

For 21 months, the Americans have been either under the watchful eye of the Japanese or penned up in a Japanese internment camp.

An American was picked by the consuls to keep the line moving, and his jibes kept them laughing as they struggled along the narrow gangplank with their bundles, suitcases, babies, banjos and baskets.

"Hold your tickets and hurry up, the boat's leaving—in three days," he urged them along.

It is expected the Gripsholm will sail late this week.

(There was no immediate explanation as to why the sailing would not come sooner, but presumably the delay was occasioned by fueling arrangements and the checking of papers.)

(The state department announced in Washington early this afternoon that the exchange of repatriates had been completed at 10 a. m., Mormugao time, without incident. The cabled notice was received by Undersecretary of State Edward R. Stettinius, Jr.)

1943

E TIMES; ROANOKE, V

GRIPSHOLM STARTS VOYAGE TO ORIENT

Exchange Liner Will Bring Back 1,250 Americans

WASHINGTON, Sept. 2 (AP).—The exchange liner Gripsholm put out from New York harbor for the Orient today, carrying with her the high hopes of relatives back home for a safe return with 1,250 American men, women and children who have been in Japanese hands since Pearl Harbor.

The big Swedish liner, made a bit less than luxurious by expansion from her usual peacetime load of some 500 passengers, had aboard 1,330 Japanese civilians who are being repatriated. Another 173 Japanese are to be picked up at Rio De Janeiro.

May Be December

On the basis of the Gripsholm's time on her first exchange trip last year, it may be early December before the Americans being brought back may walk on the free soil of their homeland again.

In the Gripsholm's hold are large quantities of relief supplies and medicines for American prisoners of war and civilians still interned in the Orient, including the Philip-

I was six years old and in first grade when we left [Daddy], nine and in fourth grade when I next saw him.

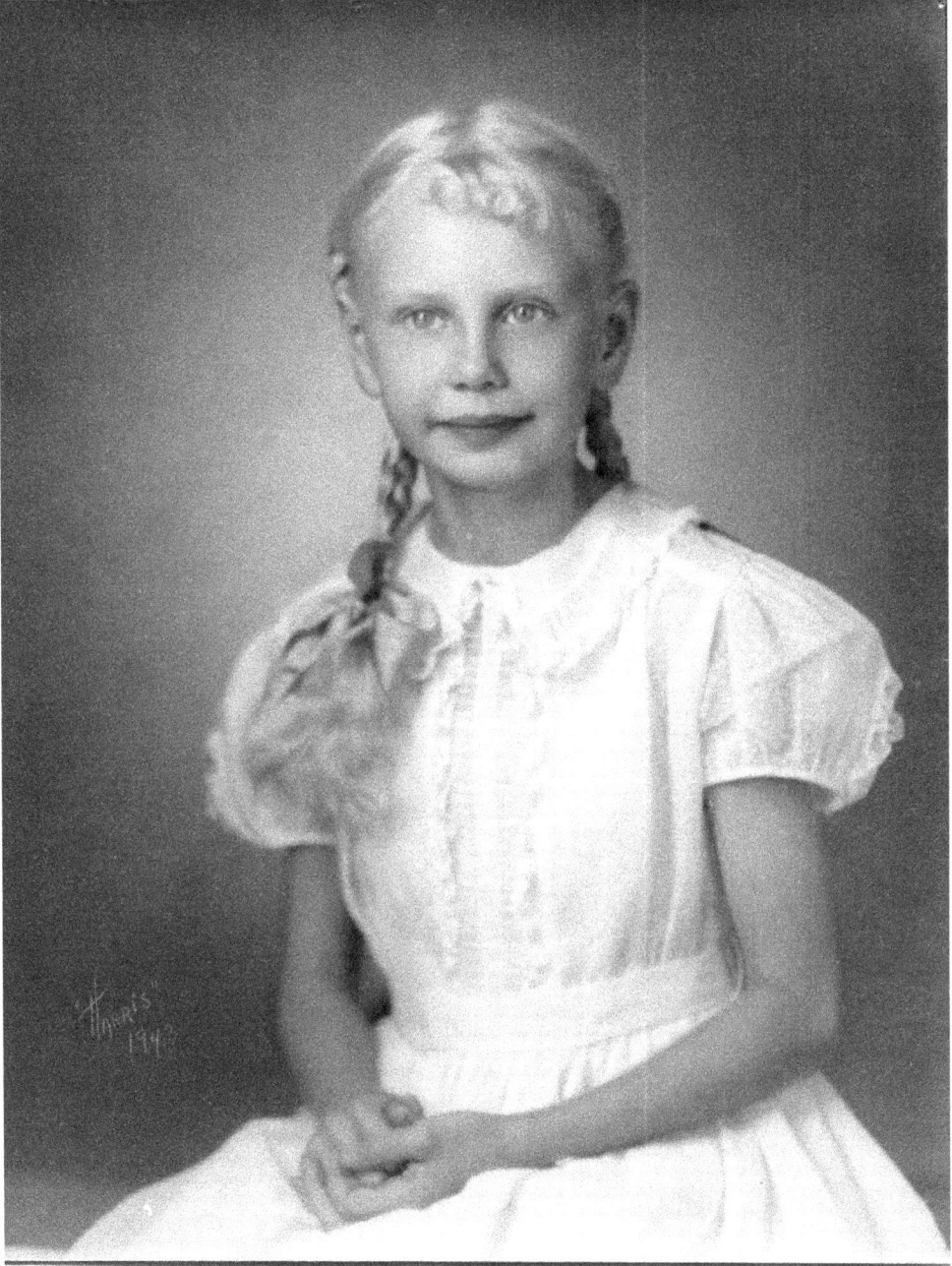

It was July 30, 1946, . . . on board the *S.S. Marchen Maersk*. After a lapse of six years we were starting the long trip back to join my father in Shanghai.

A cablegram to the ship . . . confirmed that we were relatively close to the China coast. It was addressed to Leta Tucker and simply said "Happy Birthday # Dady."

Radiotelegram Shanghai   Nr.   Ord: indl. den / 194 . Kl.

Tj. Bem.:

Adresse:
Note to Leta Tucker

Marchenmaersk

XSG

RADIO TELEGRAF

Dato: Til Station: den /   Kl.   af
                                                                                      194
Fra Station: den 31 8 1946   Kl. 2315z   af   G.
Shanghai/xsg

Modtaget:

Happy Birthday // Dady

Vedlagn
TC: Ko
Poste:
D: Iltelegram (télégr. urgent).   XP: B
RP: Svar betalt (reponse payée).
TMx: Flere Adresser (télégrammes multiples).
R. 2 (8-45 AS)

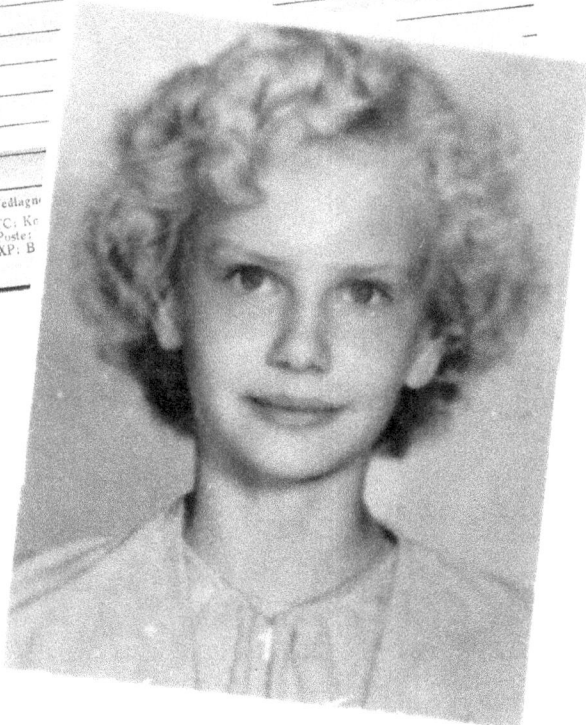

Book Three

Changes

*P*romptly at seven o'clock on our first morning back I heard a gentle tap at my bedroom door and Amah slipped in, smiling broadly.

"Time get up!" she announced.

In one hand she carried a small tray with a tall glass of steaming hot water meant for me to drink. This was a part of the British ritual of good health habits that spread to Americans as well. In the absence of fresh fruit and vegetables we were advised to drink, upon rising, a daily glass of hot water. When I hesitated, she set it on my bedside table. She then pulled out the mosquito netting tucked under the mattress, tying it in a huge knot over the bed, and turned to leave, once again reminding me it was "Time get up."

Without fail she repeated this routine, winter and summer—except in cold weather substituting a bed warmer for the mosquito net—for all the days I was in Shanghai. No need for an alarm clock. No lolling in bed either; I knew she'd be back to check. So I got up, got dressed…and drank the glass of water.

This turned out to be only one of the changes in lifestyle facing me.

I knew there would be much about China and Shanghai I would not remember; my young age and an absence of six years made this inevitable. It was inevitable, too, that this huge cosmopolitan city, only now emerging from years of war, would reflect many changes. Some held the seeds of trouble for all of us.

Two momentous changes affected the city as a whole. The Japanese were gone. No more soldiers with bayonets patrolling the streets, no more bowing to the Japanese emperor, no more Japanese in control, down in Hongkew or anywhere else. The end of the war had brought great rejoicing by everyone in the city. Many of the Chinese were grateful to the foreigners in their midst. Ricksha coolies had even offered Westerners emerging from the civilian camps free rides to their homes because "Amelica" had defeated their much detested long-time enemy. Unfortunately such a friendly spirit did not last long.

The other big change, announced to the world before the conclusion of the war, marked the end of extraterritoriality. Among the many diplomatic concessions and agreements brought about by World War II was the announcement by Generalissimo Chiang Kai Chek to Great Britain and the United States that the governing of Shanghai and the other treaty ports in China by foreign powers was no longer acceptable to the Chinese government and would not be tolerated. Trade rights belonged to China. Shanghai was to be governed by a municipal council set up by the Chinese. *Ex'trality* had been abolished. The foreign concessions as we had known them were no more.

Westerners were slow to relinquish a system that had worked successfully—at least for them—for the past hundred years. They were loath to accept any government that would directly control the super powers or any of their citizens. Familiar with the Chinese customs of retribution and financial corruption, they tried to hold back the tide of change as long as possible. But the end was near. Chinese police already patrolled the streets and many levels of Chinese bureaucrats were dispensing their own brand of "justice." Their influence and ways of governing were creeping into every level of political life, reflecting the confusion and lack of knowledge of many Chinese not used to positions of power. Underneath it all everyone knew that enough money, particularly in U.S. dollars or gold, would bring about any desired result. It was the way things had always been done in Shanghai and this would not change.

The Grosvenor House appeared much the same. The damage and destruction done by the Japanese occupation had been mostly repaired, its pre-war splendor only slightly tarnished. The Garden, though, seemed forlorn and forgotten. On sunny afternoons no flock of white-coated amahs with their eager young charges settled down on the marble terrace and steps. The great expanse of lawn Bill and I usually had to ourselves, the only ones, now, to frequent the Garden.

In our apartment one noticeable difference was the front hall closet. Only a small space was now left for hanging coats. My father had declared that he was never again going to be caught without food. The rear of the coat closet and a nook behind it had become a storage area for all kinds of canned food from baked beans to spam to canned fruit and anything in between. The shelves were already packed and were constantly being added to. This was not for everyday use but for any emergency; he was determined to be prepared. The Boy and other servants as well as Bill and I thoroughly understood the purpose.

For me the biggest change was getting used to the servants again. When Amah had appeared at the apartment within a few days of his return—having heard via the servants' grapevine that he was there—Daddy welcomed her back to her old job. Despite the changes in her duties she seemed happy to help out wherever she could. She always came when I pushed the buzzer in my room that rang in the kitchen, but I rarely used it. Much of her service now was limited to looking after my skimpy wardrobe and doing the family wash. She would bring in a pile of clean clothes, put them away and then leave me to get dressed on my own. Our relationship of years past had disappeared and I deeply regretted our inability to communicate except in general terms. There was so much I wanted to ask her. But I was grateful for all she did for me. After all, what twelve-year old would not be glad to escape making her bed every day?

Our No. 1 Boy was not our former Chang, but a new boy brought in by one of the BAT men who had lived at the apartment. An excellent cook, he fixed for breakfast whatever we requested and for other meals whatever my mother ordered or he could find at market. Since Daddy was usually home by noon on Saturdays we continued our old ritual of having "foreign" food, rather than an American meal, for lunch that day. One week it was Chinese, the next Indian, the next Russian—all of it delicious. From bird's eye soup to hundred-year-old eggs to my favorite sweet and sour pork, no Chinese food since has tasted as good as those Saturday tiffins that Boy cooked for us.

The new house coolie was Amah's nephew. When my father mentioned needing a good coolie to clean house and generally help out, she quickly mentioned her nephew. He was "velly smart," she said, and wanted to come to the city. Around nineteen years old, he was a six-foot tall, rangy northern Chinese with a shock of thick black hair, sharp black eyes, high cheek bones and a grin that came and went but usually indicated real pleasure in whatever he was doing. Daddy, knowing Amah, easily agreed to his joining the family's servants, assured that she would keep him well in hand. Proving to be highly intelligent and far above the coolie class, he nevertheless cheerfully accepted his job and did it well. Some of his duties went far beyond those of the average house coolie.

Coolie, as we called him, and Bill became great friends. Coolie was eager to learn English; Bill wanted to learn Chinese, so the two conversed in a mixture of both. Among his many talents Coolie could play the Chinese violin and at Bill's insistence on some hot summer afternoons we spent an hour or so listening to him play. These instruments are never quiet and to Western ears far from harmonious. It echoed throughout the back stairs and sounded clearly in our living room and surrounding apartments. Eventually my mother would send word that enough was enough.

Coolie could also read and write Chinese. In fact, he had received considerable schooling in his home village. Now, setting up a small table in the back servant area, near their lift, he arranged to offer a service in his spare time. He was prepared to write letters and to read correspondence to clients in need of such help. Fees for this soon became a welcome part of his income. People lined up to see him, chattering loudly, until Daddy, who had no real objection to all of this, finally told Amah that Coolie would need to find a way to limit his clientele to certain hours and to keep them quiet—which he did, setting up a kind of appointment system.

Bill and Coolie often walked down to the corner of Avenue Joffre where there was a large news stand. Here the latest American magazines were spread out on the sidewalk and tacked to the rear fence. The Chinese dealer carried recent copies of *LIFE, TIME*, the *Saturday Evening Post* and, to Bill's delight, baseball cards. If I could scrape together as much as $3,000—then one week's allowance—they would bring me back a new *Modern Screen* or *Photoplay*.

Ambition made up such a basic part of Coolie's personality that he was soon begging the chauffeur to teach him to drive our car. According to Bill, an innocent bystander, they spent much time driving into the garage, a corrugated shed provided by the apartment complex, and backing out. All went well until the day Coolie drove straight through the end of the flimsy garage into the concrete wall surrounding the compound. Fortunately the car wasn't damaged much, but the garage had to be repaired and my father informed. Coolie was always so amiable and ready to work that even Daddy didn't get too angry with him. The chauffeur was also reprimanded, but after a while the driving continued.

The chauffeur we considered another breed of Chinese altogether. Short and slight, not resembling in appearance or action the average Chinese, he apparently came from western China and had a mixed background. He spoke English fairly well, drove reasonably well and smoked cigarettes non-stop, often when driving. When our former chauffeur left for a higher office position it had proved difficult to find a replacement. My mother was convinced that this driver was a communist, probably spying on us, and not to be trusted. But we needed someone and he had acceptable credentials, so Daddy hired him—despite his rumpled appearance and tendency to smoke extra cigarettes brought home from the factory. Whether he did more than simply drive us here and there we never knew, but he seemed to know a lot of the gangs of young Chinese that crowded the streets in those days and often signaled with his fingers to greet individuals we saw at various places.

We tried to treat our servants as fairly and kindly as possible. Bill and I were expected to always be polite and respectful to each. Their duties and their wages were well within the accepted range for such positions and as the economy sank Daddy raised their pay accordingly.

Despite our suspicions about the chauffeur, we felt our servants remained loyal and seemed happy. When we moved in the spring of '48 to another, larger Grosvenor House apartment, they stayed with us. For a few weeks that summer, when we moved again into a hotel suite at Cathay Mansions, except for the Boy, who had a family to feed, they stayed available. By August, when we moved yet again to an apartment at Cavendish Court, closer to the school, along with a new Boy they went right back to their former duties.

We were very fortunate in our servants. They were not only honest but kind and cheerful and ready to do anything we asked of them. We became very fond of them, especially Amah and Coolie. They all certainly made life easier for us during these difficult postwar years in Shanghai—years filled with change.

The Flying Tigers

When my father returned to Shanghai and his BAT job in the fall of 1945, within a month of the war's end, he had two purposes in mind: to act for the BAT in preserving their China property and other assets and to reclaim our own apartment at the Grosvenor House. He and other BAT men walked back into company buildings that were barely functional, but machinery and factories were soon repaired and they were back in the production of tobacco products.

Our apartment at Grosvenor House he found in shambles. The Japs had torn out all radiators, pipes, appliances, bathroom and kitchen fixtures, and anything else that could be removed. Walls and floors were damaged and filthy. All of our furniture had disappeared except our heavy walnut dining room table and chairs, which we assumed were too high to be comfortable to the short Japanese.

To my father's great surprise he also found camping out in the almost empty Apartment 303, three of General Claire Chennault's renowned "Flying Tigers." Having flown supplies into China for months to support the military forces of Chiang Kai Shek, at the end of the war some of this unit were assigned to Shanghai. Among the first American forces to arrive in the city, they settled wherever they could find suitable quarters.

With Daddy's arrival in September the pilots quickly moved over to make room for the "rightful owner" and friendships were formed that would last for years. Their presence had really formed a kind of buffer, barring other Shanghai residents from taking over an empty apartment, thus saving it for him. These three Tigers happened to be from Texas and hit it off immediately with my father and other BAT men, all southerners, who also lived temporarily in our flat. Each pilot soon moved into his own apartment, one welcoming his wife from the States. Another, called "Skinny", was married within a few months, his bride, Tommy, flying out from Texas on a military plane and staying for several days at our apartment.

Skinny had the distinction of having helped bomb the SS *Conte Verdi*. The *Conte Verdi* was an Italian luxury liner that happened to be in the Shanghai harbor when the war started. To keep the Japs from benefiting from the huge ship, the crew scuttled it in the Whangpoo River. For the next six months or so the Japs worked hard to get it righted and renovated enough to sail again. On the day it was to leave port a lone American plane flew over and dropped a single bomb precisely in the middle of the ship. It slowly settled over again on its side. The pilots were Flying Tigers and the feat proved to be quite a morale booster, not only for the U.S. military in the Far East but also for the American internees who watched from their concentration camp across the harbor in Pootung.

Their wedding of Skinny and Tommy, coming on the heels of the war's end, was an occasion for great celebration. Tommy's long white wedding dress was made by a Chinese tailor from a silk Flying Tigers parachute. The ceremony, attended by many from that prestigious flying unit, was held at the Community Church. Daddy gave the bride away and also hosted their reception at our apartment.

The highlight of the reception was the cutting of the cake. Instead of a cake knife the bride and groom were presented with a highly polished—and cleaned!—Japanese bayonet. My father had unearthed it from some place and now he presented it with a flourish to a somewhat startled bride, who gamely used it to slice her cake, adding an original touch to the festivities. It was a gala celebration long remembered by all and fondly talked about for months. The bayonet, according to guests present, was to be saved for eventual use by my father's daughter.

One morning shortly after we returned, our parents were out shopping when the doorbell rang. Boy answered the apartment door and ushered into the living room a visitor, one of the Flying Tigers. Bill and I knew immediately who he was—Daddy had said they would probably drop by—but his six-foot plus frame, distinct insignia and the unmistakable air that pilots seemed, in those days, to carry around with them, reinforced his identity. We were thrilled to meet one of the legendary heroes we had seen in the States in newsreels at the movies, their huge planes marked by, among other decorations, the enormous sharp teeth of their namesake.

This particular Tiger was not only standing in our living room but also bearing gifts. Under one arm was a large tin of Hershey's chocolate bars and under the other two five-gallon tins of KLIM from their commissary. We were delighted especially to have the chocolate, even though it was unsweetened and needed sugar. The distinctive light yellow tins of KLIM (milk spelled backwards) brought a pleased reaction from my mother when she saw them, but only polite thanks from Bill and me. KLIM was powdered milk. Mixed with so much water (already boiled, of course) it made what resembled dairy sweet milk. To us, accustomed to the best from Virginia cows, it tasted terrible. We understood that we couldn't touch any local fresh milk, pasteurized or not, and my mother insisted that we should drink three full glasses of milk a day, so KLIM it had to be. We tried doctoring it with some of the chocolate bars, adding vanilla, stirring in powdered cocoa, piling in a spoonful of sugar—nothing made it taste any better. We ended up drinking it "straight" and after several weeks became used to it, accepting it as the mainstay of our daily meals in China.

Our Flying Tiger friend stayed only a short time on that first visit but we were to see several of them often, particularly Skinny and Paul and their wives. They quickly made us feel comfortable, regaling us with tales of their time spent in our apartment as well as some of their war adventures. They and their wives were frequently invited to dinner and on several occasions we were invited to join them at their baseball games. Here we often saw General Chennault and his Chinese wife sitting on the lower bleacher seats and actually got to meet them.

Tommy, short and shapely, with a genuine Texas drawl, we especially liked. As winter came on she suffered terribly from the unaccustomed cold. For Christmas that year Skinny presented her with "lingerie" resembling a bathing suit, hand-made by a local tailor out of soft white bunny fur. She was thrilled with it and when they visited on Christmas day insisted on modeling it for us, assuring us that it kept her "much warmer." These two Texan families, young and a lot of fun, were always welcome.

Another of our favorite visitors was Daddy's first cousin, A. P. Tucker—"Tuck." He, of course, came from Virginia and had been an important factor in Daddy's decision to join the BAT. To us he seemed almost like home folks. Though he had been interned during the war in the terrible Santa Tomas Camp in Manila, he had been on the *Gripsholm* with Daddy, and after time in the States had mostly recovered. He was back with the company in Shanghai and Nanking. Many an evening after dinner he entertained us with ghost stories and tales of his fellow college students and their pranks at William and Mary College.

"Uncle Tuck," as we called him, was awaiting the arrival of his wife, Laura, and their nineteen-year old daughter, Jean. They were in California and finding it difficult to book a suitable ship to come to China. Commercial passenger airline flights, sporadic to say the least, were long and very expensive. Like most of us they finally boarded a small freighter and after several weeks arrived in Shanghai.

The arrival of "the other Tuckers" called for much celebrating and many parties. In fact, since Jean was a pretty brunette who loved a party, it prompted the appearance on the social scene of almost all Flying Tigers who were still bachelors. Much to her parents' dismay, who thought she was too young, she fell in love with a tall, dark, and handsome Flying Tiger from Iowa. She and Bob were soon engaged and within a few months were married. The ceremony, which I attended, took place at the Community Church, with the reception held at the newly renovated Columbia Country Club. The wedding cake looked especially pretty and making its appearance again was the familiar Japanese bayonet, decorated this time with a white satin bow. It cut cake very efficiently.

The newlyweds were posted in Canton for a few months and then sent back to Shanghai, where they lived in a suite at the nearby Cathay Mansions. Mama often invited them and her parents for dinner with us. Unfortunately the marriage lasted less than a year and Jean was soon on her way back to the States.

We were among the first of the BAT families to return to Shanghai after the war and our apartment was among the first to be restored to a semblance of its prewar comfort. Daddy had had it thoroughly cleaned and painted, the beautiful wood floors refinished and some of our furniture, found in the basement, cleaned and slip-covered before we got back. We were, therefore, among the few prepared to receive visitors.

Most of the tobacco men returned soon after Daddy did, and now as suitable accommodations on ships could be found their wives and families began to arrive. Many of these were long-time friends of my parents and were eagerly welcomed back and often invited over for bridge or mah jong and dinner. Sometimes they just dropped in and stayed to eat with us. Since Boy and Coolie were on hand to provide a sumptuous meal, this was acceptable and posed no problems.

Over these first months I met many BAT people, friends and co-workers of Daddy's, as well as oil and banking friends. When they joined us for dinner, Bill and I sat enthralled with the tales they told about the Chinese and Japanese and their experiences in camp. They were always funny and entertaining; serious talk about the war was avoided. We also listened to many a song, ranging from one about the bonny banks of Scotland to several of Russian or Volga River origin and, of course, Daddy's favorite, "Carry Me Back to Ole Virginny."

Thanks largely to my father's gregarious nature and large circle of friends I got to know a wide variety of people, each of whom had his own fascinating story to tell. Certainly the most impressive of all the visitors were the dashing young Flying Tigers.

Stovepipe to the Sky

The winter of 1946-47, my first back in the city, was no colder and no wetter than many others in Shanghai. It just seemed so to those of us who lived through it. Skies loomed forever gray and sodden. Gusty winds tore around tall buildings and swept across wet pavement. Streets oozed grime and gloom. Beggars shivered in alleyways and died by the dozen on doorsteps. The city's mood, far from the soaring euphoria of immediate postwar days, had turned grim and was steadily sinking.

At 303 Grosvenor House my father, ever optimistic, was determined to make this winter more comfortable than the last. With the consent of Mr. Bashkiroff, back in his prewar position as the Grosvenor House manager, Daddy, along with assorted friends and several coolies had descended into the cavernous basement of the apartment house the previous fall to look for missing radiators, appliances and other items. They discovered a number of furnace parts, pipes and other fixtures removed by the Japs but never shipped out. Mr. Bashkiroff, somewhat intimidated by American initiative and ingenuity, as well as by the sight of several American Flying Tigers, posed no opposition when the coolies hauled up to our apartment anything needed in the way of parts for the heating system, kitchen and bathrooms, as well as some of our old appliances and furniture. Not everyone was so lucky.

While radiators in our flat were now intact, warmth was another matter. Coal was needed for the building's furnace and coal was as scarce as dragons' teeth. During that first postwar winter heat had been haphazard to say the least, with the furnace operating only two or three hours a day—some days. Now, with his family in residence, and remembering the previous cold, my father was determined that this winter would be different. He began to ponder ways to provide more heat for our apartment.

In October Mr. Bashkiroff—"that damn Russian" as my father always referred to him—sent a letter to all residents stating that the management regretted that since coal was still scarce and expensive, heat and hot water would again be rationed. Radiators would be emitting steam heat for only two hours in the morning—roughly six to eight o'clock—and two to three hours in the evening—from five to around eight o'clock. How much heat could work its way into various apartments was questionable. With our restored pipes and location on a lower floor, Daddy expected us to be better off than some, but hardly warm. As to hot water, lukewarm out of the faucet, it was to be heated on kitchen stoves and taken to respective bathtubs as the occupants needed it.

Electricity offered another avenue of heat but, charged separately to each apartment, it was extremely dear. Moreover, the wiring at Grosvenor House was of the British kind, so some electric heaters had to have separate transformers to convert 220 voltage to the American 110. Transformers as well as electric heaters were hard to find. The black market, China's perennial everyday shopping outlet, had some American heaters and someone at the factory managed to get two for Daddy, along with transformers. They could do little, however, beyond warming the bathrooms. We were still without enough heat to ward off one of Shanghai's raw, wet winters.

After much thought Daddy announced that he finally had a solution to the heating problem. On a day in November he came home from his office early, bringing with him the factory's longtime "engineer." A scruffy looking Chinese, he spoke only pidgin English. His superior knowledge and position, however, were clearly apparent in the way he flicked his wrist and used the folding wooden ruler he constantly carried with him. He spent the next hour measuring the living room, veranda and dining room, the ceilings, windows, transoms and an area in the middle of the living room floor. All the while he conversed steadily with our Boy, who listened with what at first seemed disbelief, then increasing amazement, and finally peals of laughter. When he finished measuring, he bowed to my father and left.

Daddy, it seems, had ordered the factory's chief engineer and jack of all trades to construct a heating system for the apartment—namely a stove, with necessary stovepipes and chimney. Just how this was to operate in a sixteen-floor apartment building with no fireplaces, where we were on the fourth floor, remained to be seen. Much depended, it seemed, on how a stove would "draw," but the engineer assured my father that he would make him the perfect stove.

My mother was alternately angry at my father's "foolishness" and worried that Mr. Bashkiroff would throw us out of the apartment—assuming the stove didn't burn the building down first.

"You can fuss all you want," said Daddy, "but when it turns cold and you're shivering and we have no heat, it'll be a different story."

"It will never work!" said my mother.

Had they understood English better the "engineer," Coolie and even Boy—always ready to do my father's bidding—would no doubt have agreed.

Work was to start in a few days, but in the meantime our house boy was to contact the No. 1 boy in each apartment for six floors directly above us, explain what was going on, and at specific floors ask if workers could come in to work at their outside wall. Boy returned from his mission beaming. There had been little credence that such a scheme would succeed, but no denial of access to anchor the stovepipe or even any objection to the stovepipe itself. Mr. Bashkiroff was said to be somewhat upset at rumors he had heard, but Daddy paid no attention to him.

A few days later Bill and I returned home from school to find the living room furniture moved, a small black iron stove sitting in the middle of the room and a bright, silvery tin stovepipe extending out a veranda window toward the south and a dining room window toward the north. The pipe itself was about six inches in diameter and consisted of sections four feet long that fit into each other. Here and there were various flues and elbows that would carry the pipe outside and straight up. One stretch of pipe had just been eliminated—that going out the north window—because of the constant strong wind. The workers were now concentrating only on the other pipe. Alongside the engineer, our Boy, our Coolie, and several company coolies, sat my father in his favorite role of project supervisor.

Bill and I were sent down to the Garden to check on progress. We looked up to see our Coolie hanging out the window of the eighth floor apartment, tying the stove pipe to the side of the building.

The top of the pipe had a crosspipe so the smoke would draw to each side and was fastened below any nearby windows. Grinning, Coolie waved to us and crawled back inside.

We reported back and Daddy announced that it was time for a trial run. Newspaper, wood and our few available lumps of coal were put in the stove, now anchored to a heavy metal foundation sitting on our newly refinished living room wood floor. The engineer lit a match and touched the paper. The stove filled with crackling flames. A worker hurriedly adjusted several flues. And slowly the room filled with smoke.

The engineer immediately disappeared while the rest of us doused the fire, opened every window and fanned away smoke. He soon returned to announce that changes in the stovepipe were needed. It must be made smaller in diameter—he demonstrated with his fingers—and after it angled away from our veranda window and up the wall, it should be extended four more floors past the eighth floor, above the twelve-story wing adjacent to our central building. Once the pipe was free of that wing, at the twelfth floor roof, the stove would draw perfectly, the smoke in the apartment would disappear and the fire could continue.

He left for the day to make more stovepipe. Boy went off to confer with servants on each higher floor. Daddy sat down to reassure my mother, joined now by an apprehensive Amah. Coolie, after all, was her nephew.

The next morning the engineer returned, along with several company coolies who brought up more tin stovepipe, this kind narrowing to four inches, with a new two-directional cap. After much loud talking and shouting they completed the revisions.

Bill and I again went outside to watch. The thin, shiny stovepipe now scaled the brick apartment house up to the adjacent wing's twelfth floor roof and a few feet beyond. There it swayed unsteadily in the wind. One of the coolies standing up there signaled that he was finished and left.

Inside the apartment it was time for a second trial. With everyone standing in the living room to observe, the fire flared and caught and the stove door was closed. We all watched for the first sign of smoke.

But there was no smoke! None could be seen! Or smelled!

As the fire blazed the smoke drifted through the stovepipe, making it barely warm to the touch, and seemed to be drawing perfectly up the "chimley." All the workers, chattering loudly, immediately rushed down to the Garden to observe. The engineer, elated with his accomplishment, returned to report that smoke definitely could be seen drifting out of the stovepipe. The stove was a success!

Ai yii yii!!

In the apartment my mother was warming her hands by the stove. Boy was watching the fire and chuckling to himself. Amah was wringing her hands. And Coolie, holding a bucket of water as directed, was standing by on alert—in case anything caught fire.

My father was jubilant. He immediately called in Boy and gave him a handful of *cumsha* (extra money) for himself, our Coolie, the head engineer and his entourage. Then, though it was early in the afternoon, he told the Boy to bring him his customary bourbon and water and he immediately toasted the stove.

Coolie was placed in charge of the heating system. He was to clean and polish the stove every morning, add fuel to keep the fire burning, bank it every night and maintain a bucket of water nearby for safety purposes. He was also to keep an eye on the stovepipe outside and make any needed repairs. The chauffeur was to be told when the fuel supply was dwindling; he in turn would inform the engineer at the factory, who would deliver whatever was available to burn, hopefully some coal.

All winter when Bill and I awoke to freezing temperatures and clanking radiators cool to the touch, it was reassuring to throw on our clothes and warm ourselves at the stove as we ate breakfast and got ready for school. It was also a comfort whenever we came in from outside. Even my mother conceded that the stove saved us that winter. My father unceasingly reminded us of the brilliance of his plan, accepted congratulations from our many visitors who dropped in to see it, and frequently toasted with bourbon and water the snug little stove in the middle of the living room floor.

Until warm weather arrived in the spring we kept a fire going in the stove. Whenever I was down in the Garden I always checked out the shiny tin pipe bravely climbing the brick wall of the tall apartment building. Usually, if the light was right, I could just make out a thin wisp of smoke drifting from the stovepipe out into the sky.

From Ricksha to Pedicab

$\mathcal{W}$here were all the rickshas? Though they hadn't completely disappeared, they sometimes were hard to find. Where once Amah and I had ridden home from school in a ricksha, now Bill and I relied on the pedicab.

On the main streets the "new" pedicabs were everywhere. While its role was similar to the ricksha's, the pedicab, a kind of ricksha and bicycle combination, was becoming more and more popular. To some it resembled a large tricycle, with a double passenger seat toward the back anchored to the rear wheels, making the whole vehicle steady on the ground. The coolie sat on a bicycle seat in front and pedaled, guiding the wheel in front of him.

The pedicab, everyone said, was quicker, easier on the coolie driver, more "humane," and offered a speedier and more comfortable means of transportation than the old-fashioned ricksha. It certainly seemed the more modern, up-to-date and sophisticated way— except for a chauffeured automobile—to get around Shanghai. The ricksha, though still seen, began to fade into the background and to serve predominantly older customers and those with less cash.

Most pedicabs operated through a system of managers who owned several cabs and rented them out to drivers. They staked out territory and set the fares. The drivers were dependent, of course, on finding a customer wishing a ride. Therefore anyone approaching on foot down a nearby street provided a golden opportunity for any driver to go into action and eventually collect a fare.

"Pedicab, Missy? Velly clean."

"Masta want pedicab? Velly fast."

The pleas to customers brought varied results. The prospective fare usually chose the cleanest white cushions and the coolie who seemed to know enough English to get him where he wanted to go.

For most of one year Bill and I rode a pedicab home from school. Each morning our chauffeur—or for a while a BAT company car serving as a bus for several children—took us out to school and then drove our father the six or seven miles to his office. With shortages in gasoline and high prices, though, it wasn't feasible for him to return for us when school dismissed around one o'clock. The obvious solution lay in the pedicab.

Our Boy assured Daddy that he had a reliable friend who owned his own vehicle. He would meet us at the school's front entrance each day and drive us home. We went out back to look at the coolie and then he and Boy finalized the necessary financial arrangements.

On the first day we were to ride the pedicab home, Bill and I walked out the school's front gate to confront a half dozen pedicabs. All clamoring for the fare, their drivers, to us, all looked alike. One, however, pushed ahead toward us and somehow convinced us that he was our driver. We climbed in. He started out at a steady pace down Petain Lu, but then turned off down another, unfamiliar street. I began to grow uneasy. Here we were, two young, vulnerable

Americans, unable to speak Chinese, unfamiliar with this route and unsure of our driver. Not until we reached a recognizable section of Avenue Joffre and turned in at the Grosvenor House compound did I relax. Each day our driver faithfully appeared at the school's front gate and after a while we recognized "our" coolie. At my request, though, Boy instructed him to come home by the more familiar route.

On bright, warm sunshiny days riding in the pedicab was a real pleasure for us, weary from school and hungry for lunch. But that winter it seemed to rain almost every day—rain in torrents. For this development the pedicab's accordion-type roof was raised, stretching over our heads, and a heavy black oil cloth was hooked to each side and draped over the foot rest. This left us enveloped inside a black, rubbery, smelly, tent-like enclosure, unable to see out. Water dribbled through several weak spots in the roof and streamed down cracks, often getting us wet. The pedals squeaked loudly with each turn while rain beat down on the top and trickled off the front coverings under which we were buried. At the Grosvenor House entrance the wind, as usual, whipped around us, often dislodging the oil sheets and blowing rain in on us. On those days it was a relief to get home. On sunny days we enjoyed a pleasant drive in an open pedicab with much to see along the way.

Though we couldn't speak each other's language we even became friends, of a sort, with the pedicab coolie. At the end of the school year we thanked him for his help and asked Daddy to give him plenty of *cumsha*, which he accepted with a big grin.

We never saw him again, at least to our knowledge. But he probably was one of the crowd of coolies who frequented nearby Avenue Joffre, where many a prospective customer might answer the call of "Pedicab, Missy?"

Shanghai American School

$\mathcal{T}$o all of us who ever attended it there was something special about the Shanghai American School. From the first time I walked past the tall flagpole at the main entrance, through its heavy wrought iron front gate and inside the high bamboo fence surrounding the campus, I sensed that this was an exceptional place. I felt privileged to be one its students, honored to be a part of it.

This was, indeed, no ordinary school, but *the* American School in Shanghai. Before the war it held a reputation as the best American educational institution outside of the continental United States. Its academic standing had been excellent—on a par with California schools, then the nation's finest, and in some ways even exceeding that standard. Its graduates had attended the most prestigious colleges and universities in the United States and throughout the world.

The American community in postwar Shanghai welcomed the announcement by its board that the school would open in the fall of 1946. The goal, as always, would be to provide the best education possible for American children in this foreign city. My father immediately contacted the principal's office to enroll my brother and me in the third and seventh grades and to make the necessary tuition payments. I was, in a way, a returning student, since for a few weeks before the 1940 evacuation I had attended first grade. Others were in the same category.

The opening day was set for September 24. For the time being classes were to be held during an extended morning session; later there would also be afternoon classes. While at first the administration had aimed only for grades one through ten, with additional advanced studies on an individual basis, they soon recognized the need for a full high school program. I entered the seventh grade along with around twenty classmates; the number would fluctuate over the months as a few left and others arrived. The senior class claimed thirty-three, the eighth grade thirty-six and the seventh grade eventually would match them. The total school enrollment for 1946-47 was set at three hundred eighty-five; by the following year it had increased to well over four hundred. The staff and faculty numbered forty-one.

We, the first students to enter the school upon its formal reorganization after the war, were faced with a unique challenge: to restore the school's reputation for academic excellence and high moral values and to make it once more shine. The mantle laid upon us stretched back to 1912 when the school first began, through 1923 when the new campus was acquired and the present buildings on Avenue Petain opened, past the occupation of World War II days to the present postwar effort. Everyone who had known it before the war was watching closely. Most of us were well aware of the interest and hopes for success that accompanied us on that opening day of school.

At our first school assembly—for grades seven through twelve—we were welcomed by our principal, Mr. Gibb, several board members and a special guest speaker, the United States Ambassador to China, the Honorable J. Leighton Stuart. In his remarks he, too, reminded us of the importance of the school, adding words of encouragement and good wishes for a successful school year and a return to its former state of excellence. He assured us that we were up to the challenge. Over the coming months others echoed his words of encouragement including members of the Board of Directors and guests such as the Honorable H. H. Kung, treasurer of China, and General Claire Chennault of the Flying Tigers.

With its colonial architecture, red brick Georgian buildings with white trim, and wide green lawns the school seemed a bit of America set down on this foreign soil, offering all of us a little piece of home. The physical layout was not only extensive but also attractive. The large administration and classroom building, the girls' dormitory, the boys' dormitory, the dining room and music building, the gymnasium, football, soccer and hockey fields, a brick water tower and connecting walks and colonnades rivaled many a small American college campus.

Taken over by Japanese during the war, the entire school had been used for some of their purposes. Now it had been cleaned, painted and refurbished before it reopened. Many old furnishings, stored in the attic, were put back to use. Science labs, though lacking in modern equipment, were gradually improved and old textbooks updated as they could acquire them. A larger, more modern gymnasium was built, in anticipation of a thorough sports program, and everything else, including the curriculum, brought as up to date as possible. The building and the grounds were always kept in pristine condition, thanks to the Chinese staff hired to keep it so.

Since there were so few of us in each class we all knew each other, especially in this first year. Only nine or ten girls enrolled initially in the seventh grade and about the same number of boys. For our English and history classes boys and girls were taught separately; the science and math classes were combined. I never understood the thinking behind this but always felt that we learned more when we were divided by gender. Accustomed to staying in the background, the girls by themselves felt freer to speak their minds and were listened to more readily. With the boys, at that age, there seemed to be more confusion and misbehavior. Seventh grade math and science suffered, and for me were never particularly enjoyable subjects.

My favorite class was always history. For the seventh grade it was to be the history of China. We met right after morning roll call, in a large, rather dark classroom furnished with a half dozen heavy wood tables with six or eight matching chairs around each. The Chinese were excused from this class to take a class in English speech. The remaining six or seven girls sat around one table with the teacher at the head.

Our teacher was Captain Edmund Wilkes, recently of the U.S. Army. A graduate of Harvard University with master's courses to his credit, he was a bachelor around forty years old, balding and wearing glasses, with a soft voice and kind eyes. He called each of us "Miss" with our last name and from the first hour he charmed us all. A strict grader and disciplinarian, he demanded the best we could give and had a way of treating each of us as a respected, unique and valued individual. This course, on a par with some college courses I later took, presented a fascinating, challenging and thorough survey of centuries of Chinese history and culture. One of the best teachers I ever had, he made it memorable.

I especially enjoyed the question and discussion periods that dominated our class time. We often wound up in informal debates over various aspects of the course. Some topics were selected from our out-dated text; more came from Mr. Wilkes's own observations of the Chinese people. One discussion covered the horrors of the Japanese occupation of Shanghai and Nanking. Since the Chinese practiced numerous religions, we spent time comparing Taoism, Confucianism and Buddhism with Christianity. On another day we explored the Koran.

All of our class time was not spent on history per se but also on Chinese culture; art held a special place on the schedule and became a favorite topic. Every week or so we would find, usually sitting in the middle of the table, a beautiful porcelain vase, a scroll of Chinese calligraphy, a Ming Dynasty bowl, a delicate water color of the Yangtze River gorges or a carved statue of the goddess Kwan Yin. These were no "tourist" pieces; they were genuine works of art, either owned by Mr. Wilkes or loaned to him by friends of the school. Available for us to examine in detail, we were also graded on our knowledge in this area. I had always loved history, but Mr. Wilkes showed me its beauty and significance. The insight I gained from his teaching broadened my outlook as a person, led me to teach history and strengthened a love of the subject that would last a lifetime.

Another of my teachers who stands out as excellent I had my freshman year for Latin I. Her name was Evelyn Merritt and all of us, at least for some weeks, were scared to death of her. Bowlegged, sturdy and strong, she stood no taller than five feet and wore her faded red hair in a plait across her head. Probably in her late thirties, she had a large Roman nose and small beady eyes that bored through you to examine every bit of Latin you ever thought you knew. She was British, with high academic credentials from both a university at Liverpool and Oxford University. She knew Latin backwards and forwards, along with math, Shakespeare and English literature. Every day as soon as the bell rang we had a short quiz, in our case usually ten vocabulary words or short Latin phrases. Every day the quiz from the day before was returned with a numerical grade and sometimes a succinct remark at the top of the page—all written in bright green ink. I valued more than I can say those tiny green "100"s I earned from this superb teacher.

Report cards came out twice a semester. They were not given to us, but mailed to our parents at home. A one-page form letter with grades, usually numerical, along with a detailed comment from each teacher, it was typed in the office. My name had somehow been misspelled in the main office—with an "e" for May—and despite specific requests and numerous explanations to teachers with their roll books, it never seemed to get corrected. I finally gave up asking but continued to sign all homework and test papers with the correct—and very clear—spelling of my name.

School was very important to me. The routine of attending classes was a comforting part of my everyday life in this foreign world. School was, in fact, the grounding factor in my life, for there was little else for me to do with my time. It was one of the few things that could compare with life back in the States. Despite petty squabbles among my classmates, anxiety over giving reports and writing papers, and a driving need to make high grades, I enjoyed it. I might be chauffeured by car to the campus every morning and driven home in a pedicab by a Chinese coolie, but once on campus I was on my own in an almost-American world, with a routine familiar in many ways.

The success of SAS, sometimes in adverse circumstances, was in no small part due to its strong faculty and administration, but also to its exceptional student body. As students we were well served by this very special institution. My academic career was greatly influenced by my years there. We all had good cause to be grateful for the splendid opportunities opened to us through the Shanghai American School.

Friends

*A*s beautiful as the SAS campus was, and as capable and helpful as were the teachers, it was the students who interested me the most.

As in the past, many were children of American missionaries. Some whose parents served in the interior of China attended the school as boarders, but the dormitories were far from full in this first postwar term. Surprisingly, a few of these "mish kids" had never even been to the States; they had remained in China during the war, been interned and would go to America when they were ready for college.

Another large group consisted of children of American businessmen—those connected with the consular service, banking, tobacco, oil and trade. There were as well a number of children of U.S. military forces stationed in Shanghai since the end of the war. To most of us this was "our" school—it belonged to all of us. There were no ruling "cliques," none who for one reason or another were superior to others. For the first time in my life I was attending a school where I belonged as much as any of the other students.

Not all who enrolled were Americans. A number of sons and daughters of wealthy Chinese attended, students hoping to someday study in the United States or whose fathers held high positions in Chiang Kai Shek's government. Russian, German and Jewish students whose families could afford the tuition, instead of the Jewish, French or British institutions chose the American school. Some students were Eurasian—of mixed background—or the children of Chinese and American parents. A number were "stateless"—Russians, mainly Tzarist supporters whose parents escaped the communist takeover of their country, or Jews who fled from Nazi Germany in the '30s, or those born in Shanghai of immigrant parents. Many had no passport or tie to any country, a dangerous position to be in, but permissible—indeed, common—in Shanghai. Some of our most talented and creative fellow students fell into these categories, giving us all a disregard for some of the world's political distinctions and a deep respect for the individual.

While many of us differed in visible ways, one thing was evident: almost all who attended were academically and intellectually above average, with the discipline and desire to do well. There were exceptions, particularly among seventh and eighth grade boys who for a while had difficulty in settling down to school, but by far the majority valued highly this opportunity to get a superior education and worked hard to achieve it.

We all held an obvious bond in the English language since most spoke it fluently. Some, particularly the missionary kids, also spoke the Chinese dialect common to the area where they had lived. Chinese spoke their native Chinese, while children of Germans, Russians or Spanish spoke their parents' language. All learned to speak, read and write English with excellence.

Many of the students held another common bond. This was their love for classical music. It was almost a second language for many. Americans as a whole didn't fall into this category, but those students who grew up in China as a rule had studied either piano or violin as small children and continued their lessons as they grew older. Especially was this true of those of European background, as well as the upper class Chinese. Through family custom they held a respect and appreciation for classical music not gained from phonograph records, for these were scarce, but from their own ability to play and enjoy their chosen instrument. Everyone, whether playing an instrument or not, developed a love and respect for classical music and for the time and talent involved in studying it. Athletic ability was valued, particularly by Americans, but of equal value—if not higher consideration—was the love for and appreciation of music.

Among my friends in seventh grade was Ann, who lived for a short time at Grosvenor House. She came from Ithaca, New York. Why she remained my friend I don't quite know, for she seemed to ridicule everything I did. Mainly she accused me and my Virginia family of still "keeping slaves." Shocked at what I considered ignorance, I was put on the defensive and felt this affected our entire friendship although we sometimes went to movies together, rode to school together and even spent the day at each other's homes. I was as much puzzled as hurt at some of her accusations for at times they were expressed in our class discussions; my southern accent brought criticism along with my whole southern background. I shall always remember her fondly, though, because of a special gift she gave me for Christmas that year—a set of four small porcelain T'ang Dynasty horses, a lovely example of Chinese art and, indeed, a reminder of our shared Chinese history class. Despite our differences we were still friends when she left China at the end of seventh grade.

I was in the minority and on the defensive for other reasons. Since some of my peers were missionary children the fact that my father was "tobacco" and manufactured "sinful" cigarettes brought out other prejudice. This was not true of everyone but even one of my teachers, a middle-aged American long in China, gave me the distinct impression that I was not to be considered in the same light as the "mish kids," her main concern and regarded as far superior. Fortunately this was only true of one teacher; most were fair and displayed no such bias. Certainly the missionary kids were not in the majority, nor were they academically superior to the rest of us.

Among my classmates several stood out as special. SiSi Chu, tall, thin and willowy, with short, cropped black hair and large smiling black eyes was one of the Chinese in my class. She was quiet and rarely said much, but spoke English perfectly and knew more about mathematics than any girl I had ever encountered. Another was short and pudgy and a little harder to get to know. Rumor had it that she was the daughter of a high government official considered one of the wealthiest Chinese in the country.

Felicity C., whose first name I had never heard but especially liked, seemed typical of her New England heritage, quietly following her chosen way. Another friend hailed from Mississippi. Conscientious, straitlaced and never in doubt between black and white, she often made the rest of us examine our own beliefs and rethink our ideas. Despite our common Southern background she and I had our differences.

Two of my closest friends had had polio as small children; they wore braces and used crutches. Sarah was a missionary's daughter but much more broad minded than most, friendly and open to everyone. She was a year ahead of me but we had much in common. She, Annie and I spent many a summer afternoon together, talking about books, music and other things of mutual interest.

Annie, though, was my best friend. Her mother, an American nurse from Pennsylvania, worked with missionaries. Her father, a Chinese doctor specializing in tuberculosis, was regarded as one of the top men in his field in China. They lived in a small house in the compound of a Chinese T.B. hospital.

The first time I visited in her home I was shocked at its barrenness. There was little furniture and only the barest of necessities. But sitting on the floor of her bedroom was a small borrowed phonograph and as I walked into the room I was surrounded by the rising wail of George Gershwin's "Rhapsody in Blue." It was a moment of beauty I have never forgotten. Certainly I had no phonograph nor access to such beautiful music.

Annie and I shared all of our classes and many a confidence over the time we knew each other. In many ways she was my mainstay for my years at SAS, a true friend. Sometimes on Saturday nights when my parents were out I invited her for supper. She would bring her violin and we would try to play duets—not too successfully. Then we just sat and talked until she was driven home about eight.

There were no places we could meet and simply visit, have something to eat or even shop—this was not done. During the summer after seventh grade, though, we were able to go to "The Shack." Many years before, or so it seemed, I had viewed it as a benign little cottage, the site of my first grade classroom. Now, seven years later, I saw it again as the center of the school's primitive summer recreation effort. Open two afternoons a week under the watchful eye of Miss Schiff, a member of the administrative staff assigned to be chaperone, it was available as a gathering place in the summer for those students living in the city. There was no formal "program." We played cards and other games—if someone remembered to bring them from home—slaughtered ping pong, drank cokes, sang songs and played the piano. It wasn't much, but it did help relieve the boredom. Annie and I and another dozen or so gathered each afternoon it was open by the old bamboo gate.

On many Sundays during my two and a half years in Shanghai Annie and I along with other day students and boarders attended the Community Church. Across Avenue Petain from SAS the church was closely associated with the school. It was a lovely stone gothic building covered with ivy, resembling many in the States and, apparently, in England. The sanctuary featured dark wood— pews and walls and finishing touches. It presented a sense of quiet dignity and reverence that promoted a sense of worship. We students, usually sitting together, loved singing the familiar hymns and following the same service many of us had known back home. "Oh God, our help in ages past. . ." sounded just as powerful in China as it ever had in Virginia.

The church also provided another means of social get-togethers in the form of the Youth Fellowship. We all went faithfully every Sunday evening, enjoying a simple meal, discussions and programs, square dancing and a chance to get to know other students.

Friends were important to all of us. There were the expected spats and disagreements among some, but in general we all held a strong attachment to each other simply because we were all students at SAS.

Polonaise in Chinese

$\mathcal{W}$hen I read in the *Shanghai Evening Post* that the 1945 movie version of the life of Frederick Chopin, "A Song to Remember," would soon be playing at the Cathay Theatre down at the corner of Avenue Joffre, I was determined to see it. Familiar melodies began at once to float through my mind. It would be, I knew, a movie to remember.

When we had left the States the year before, this movie's theme song was playing on every radio station in the country and had soared to the top of what was called the record scene. Based on Chopin's "Polonaise in A Flat," the popular version was titled "'Til the End of Time" and it quickly became one of my favorites. Hollywood's postwar output of musical biographies of great composers included a movie on George Gershwin that I had seen, and one on Rachmaninoff, that I missed by two days. Chopin's was a must.

I was twelve years old and had been taking piano lessons since I was seven. Now, at the Shanghai American School, I spent two half-hour sessions each week "studying the piano" with Miss Olga Keuter, a Russian spinster lady of impeccable musical credentials—she had even studied at the Paris Conservatory.

"Practice! Practice! Practice!" was Miss Keuter's constant cry to me. And I did—at least the required two hours every afternoon. To play Chopin became a goal most desirable and not, I thought, impossible. The movie, I told myself, would be my reward for those long hours of mindless scales.

Getting to the movie, however, was not going to be easy. In Shanghai it was not the kind of activity that a young girl, or even two or three in a group, could attend alone. Arrangements had to be made. A chaperone was imperative. Someone had to go with me. My friend Ann, whose parents had taken us to other movies, was currently, for some reason, mad at me—a frequent development that annoyed me no end—but she was not particularly musical anyway. Knowing my mother and father, the latter inclined to Laurel and Hardy, Abbot and Costello, I was a little worried. Could I go? I posed the question first to my mother, then to my father. Over the next several days I persisted.

At first the answer was a vague "maybe." Declining to go themselves they at last agreed to let me go, provided Amah went with me. Considerable further discussion followed regarding Bill, whose presence at this movie I decidedly did not want, and whether he might as well go, too. Finally we reached a compromise of sorts. He went to visit a friend and I, despite my reluctance, went to the matinee with Amah.

How I longed for Virginia and a small town Saturday night picture show.

The next afternoon promptly at two-fifteen we started out. I led the way, with Amah at my elbow—not companions, but Young

Missy and chaperone. Close behind us followed Coolie. Making our way past swanky dress shops and expensive shoe salons, we walked the half-block from our apartment to the Cathay Theater at the corner of Avenue Joffre, a wide, busy street thick with traffic. Immediately the throng of beggars who worked that corner closed in around us, moving along with us to the theater.

Coolie headed for the entrance to negotiate the ticket-buying, an act of assertion thought to be more than I, speaking no Chinese, or Amah, being of shy and timid nature, was capable of handling. Giving the tickets to Amah, Coolie turned with a grin and a wave and started back home. She and I got in line beside huge wall posters of the show's stars, Cornel Wilde and Merle Oberon, their enormous, locally-rendered portraits each bearing a faintly Oriental look.

The theater, once luxurious and up to date, now seemed little more than a large bare barn. The floor was concrete, hard and cold. The heating was sparse, if any such system was even in operation, and the narrow wood seats were unpadded and uncomfortable. I chose to sit at the front of the back section, toward the middle, with an excellent view of the screen. We were in plenty of time and settled in to wait. Entertaining us in the meantime were recordings of Chinese violin music. The acoustics, I could tell, were not any more sophisticated than the rest of our surroundings. Gradually the seats around us filled, mostly with Chinese.

Since it was chilly and I had been down with a cold, Amah, sitting at my left, rummaged through the large basket she had brought with her and drew out a wool afghan, tucking it tightly around me. Then she pulled out her knitting—Chinese women are never without their knitting—and settled back in her seat to survey the crowd in the semi-darkness. I don't think this was the first movie she had ever attended, but no abacus was needed to figure the total.

I could tell she was a little nervous. Of Chopin's identity she would have not the remotest idea and she would not know much more by the time she left because she would not be able to read the Chinese subtitles flitting along one side of the screen.

Soon the violin stopped, the screen lit up and we plunged into 19th century Poland. I was at once enthralled by story, scenery, costumes—and music. Etudes, waltzes and mazurkas spilled into my ears and soul. Never had I heard such beautiful music. The "Polonaise" pulsed with the cause of Polish freedom and echoed its melody throughout the many maladies of its composer's life. Caught up again in the magic of a good movie I was entranced. I sank deeper into the warm afghan and further under the spell cast by the movie.

It soon became increasingly difficult, however, to ignore the static in my state of bliss. People, talking all the while, moved in and out of seats, up and down the rows, and back and forth in the aisles. Some even stood in front of my seat; in order to see I had to crane my neck around someone blocking the screen.

Babies cried and were shushed. Food, carried in covered bamboo baskets, suddenly appeared and the sounds of eating were audible in every direction. The scent of garlic—that staple of Chinese diet and health—slowly clouded the air, almost suffocating me with its pungent aroma. A host of knitting needles on all sides began to click in time to Chopin's piano. And every few minutes Amah gazed with concern—or, as the plot thickened, with alarm—at my face.

On the screen, with smoldering countenance, Cornel Wilde contemplated a jar of dirt from his Polish homeland. Behind me Chinese voices explained aloud and at length the fine points of this "foreign cinema" plot. In vivid technicolor the romance of Chopin and Sand rose to full crescendo; in chilly reality Amah reached over to rub my cold legs and tighten the afghan around me. In scene after poignant scene, while Frederick wasted away with disease, the crashing chords of the "Polonaise" became louder and more passionate. Tears filled my eyes, rolled down my cheeks and into my handkerchief.

Suddenly Amah leaned over and, peering closely up in my face, pulled my eyes away from the screen.

"You sad?" she whispered. "You want go home?"

I groaned. The spell was broken. The magic disintegrated. I shook my head and stifled a sob of frustration, my adolescent heart crushed.

In a few minutes the movie ended, the lights went up and the screeching Chinese violin started up again. Laughing and chattering loudly, most of the audience gathered up knitting, food and babies and moved toward the door. Others, having paid once and not required to leave yet, remained to eat.

Amah and I walked home in silence. I stewed over my plight. At every movie I attended now, would Amah be hovering over me? Surely there was another way to do this.

I knew my mother would ask about the afternoon. I mulled over what I would say. It was a lovely movie. The story and the scenery and especially the music had been beautiful. I was so glad I had gone.

But never again would I hear Chopin's "Polonaise" and not think of Amah. *She* was the song I would remember.

Of Small Things Not Forgotten

Christmas Day, 1946 was like no other that I would ever know. It was probably the last of its kind, too, for many inhabitants of Shanghai. Following the custom established years before, particularly among the British, presents began to pour into our apartment days ahead of time from the Chinese and Russians associated with my father's factory. Early arrivals included four chickens, one turkey, one ham, a slab of bacon, one dozen oranges, a cake, a two foot by two foot box of candy, ten dozen eggs and, probably the most appreciated, two sacks of coal.

For the Day itself, also according to custom, my parents were planning an open house. The entire household began to get ready, finding a place to put the numerous gifts and preparing the necessary refreshments. One of the main requirements for the latter was, according to my father, an ample supply of egg nog. Gallons would be needed. Daddy set out to prepare it, with the help of Boy and Coolie. They used, among other assorted ingredients, one hundred fifteen eggs, some kind of whipped cream, six bottles of brandy and three bottles of rum. Bill and I were forbidden to even taste it. Daddy declared it to be excellent.

Our apartment was decorated for the season with several pots of poinsettias and a small tree, very expensive at four US dollars. We decorated it with ornaments brought from home and some tinsel donated by friends. It looked bright, festive and very American.

Meanwhile more gifts were accumulating: ten boxes of candy, two neckties, two woolen handmade scarves, two large blue satin pillows embroidered with gold dragons, a pair of cerise pillows decorated with flowers, a dozen silver plated teaspoons, a bolt of white silk, a silver dresser set, and two more live chickens along with a card reading "To Dad on Father's Day."

At nine-thirty on Christmas morning visitors began filing in. Most could speak no English. In general they came in, greeted my parents, presented any gifts they still had, stood around smiling, drank a little of the foreign brew they were offered and left. Bill and I, after grasping the situation, faded into the background, trying to stay out of sight.

By two o'clock that afternoon over ninety guests had come and gone. Around two-fifteen the family sat down to a traditional Christmas dinner—mostly American but with a few British touches. We had as company several friends of my parents whose wives had still not come back to China. It was a fun, enjoyable dinner.

It had been a cold, foggy day. That evening we became aware of the constant drone of several airplanes flying overhead. Within the next few hours three passenger planes, with no available instruments for "blind landings," crashed on landing at Shanghai's Hungjao Airport. All aboard each plane were killed. Among them were a former Flying Tiger whose wife was on her way to China and two young boys that Bill and I knew slightly. It was a tragic ending to an already strange and, for me, unorthodox Christmas Day.

*P*ale sunlight on this late winter afternoon lit up the Whangpoo as we headed up river for Pootung and the Shanghai harbor. My family and I, along with several other guests, were returning from a visit down the Yangtze to the Texas Oil Company's installation plant on the river. A Texas Oil friend from Virginia and his Australian wife, Madeline, had invited us for a leisurely day at their newly assigned post. They had recently been moved from Shanghai to the Yangtze compound where their company had its large refineries and homes for three or four foreign managers and their families.

Their modern house, extensively redecorated, sat on a high flat bluff beside the river. Marring the view in some places stood various buildings and huge oil tanks, but their home and nearby garden provided a clear, beautiful view of the Yangtze. We toured the compound, Bill and I being particularly interested in the variety of animals; we counted thirty rabbits, numerous chickens and turkeys, four cats and one lone dog. We enjoyed delicious Chinese chow for tiffin and then settled down at the large windows in their living room to watch the activity on the river.

Madeline at first had resented this move and almost refused to go, but she finally relented and, despite some loneliness, now raved about the easy life—thanks to their several Chinese servants—and the beauty of the river. They could easily have been British colonial settlers of a century past, sent to some isolated, undeveloped area of China to make their home, promote the success of their company and bring to the Chinese the wonders of western civilization.

Now, in the late afternoon of a cold but not unpleasant day, we were returning up river on their launch. Heavy river traffic near this large, international city surrounded us on every side. The variety of ships sailing to and from the Shanghai harbor never ceased to interest me so I stayed on deck to watch.

As we had entered the Whangpoo near Woosung I had noticed a Chinese junk trailing behind us. The large wooden vessel glided steadily toward us in the soupy, muddy water, its towering stiff sails glinting blood-brown in the faint sunlight. Moving silently, nearing our launch, it suddenly filled the horizon, a commanding presence at home on its river.

I watched, fascinated, as the junk, dominating the river traffic, relentlessly pursued its path. Though at first it had drifted behind us, now it moved much closer. Menacing in its somber darkness, it suddenly drew even with us, blocking the winter sunset with its bulk. Dust and dirt from countless years coated its dingy, weathered deck and caked the crevices of its brittle, unbending sails. Everything on it, cloaked in layers of grime, seemed drab, dreary and dark—and in its silence somehow sinister.

Below deck, extending out of small portholes, a half-dozen oars padded with old rags swished steadily up and down, sounding a muffled *creak-sh, creak-sh.* It made no other sound. No flag waved, no voice called, no face could be seen. As if somehow guided by all who had ever sailed it, the junk seemed wrapped in a forlorn, disdainful solitude.

From deep within its hold an aged, heavy beam groaned once— and then again. With a sudden roll the vessel shuddered and heaved past us. Determined, it lurched even farther in front of us, unseen eyes propelling it along its way. Majestic in its bearing despite its primitive operation, it surged past the harbor ships. Arrogant in its inferiority, yet threatening even in its weakness, it slipped into the river shadows ahead—regal and remote, resenting our presence.

As I watched, it disappeared in the growing darkness. All the pride of an ancient people sailed with it, surrounding it with the fortitude and resilience of hundreds of years of effort and perseverance. I gazed at the haunting beauty of this junk, seeing in it the unfathomable mystery that is China.

*F*irecrackers in all their splendor have always been associated with Chinese celebrations. Firecrackers, too, made my thirteenth birthday special.

It had been another hot August day, one of a humid, suffocating heat wave. After a delicious birthday dinner I had opened my presents. My favorite was a delicate sandalwood Chinese fan, decorated with flowers on a green background. It looked and smelled so delicious.

Because of the heat many residents of the Grosvenor House had descended into the Garden in the early evening, hoping to catch a stray breeze or two. My father suggested we all go out, too, so we settled ourselves in chairs brought down by Coolie and placed on the higher grassy terrace at the far side of the garden.

Daddy then decided we needed firecrackers to celebrate my thirteen years and dispatched Boy and Coolie to buy some. They soon returned with a varied supply and proceeded to set them off in the Garden. Mr. Bashkiroff, "that damn Russian," immediately sent word that this was not allowed on the premises. Daddy, as usual, ignored him.

All of the firecrackers went off as expected, loud and bright against the darkening sky. The last one was spectacular: an enormous red Chinese dragon that overshadowed the entire garden. Its fire-breathing nostrils and long tail, explained Boy later, were symbols of good luck meant especially for me and my coming year.

A smattering of applause followed the display and Coolie, after a quick bow, disappeared into the building. Mr. Bashkiroff loomed large in the lighted ground floor doorway as many residents began to trail back inside to their apartments. Too late to stop the show, he soon withdrew.

Daddy, too, finally decided it was time for us to call it a night. But not before I had enjoyed my own unique celebration with firecrackers that would be unmatched at any other of my many birthdays.

$\mathcal{A}$mah, as the servant now with the most seniority among our household staff, oversaw everything that went on. She was particularly pleased at the arrival of Coolie upon the domestic scene and at the success of his various endeavors. Soon she was seeking to further the career of the Coolie's sister, her niece.

The niece was invited to Shanghai to visit. A chubby young woman around eighteen, with thick, shiny black braids, she was hoping for a job in the big city. Amah told us what she was doing and asked permission for her niece to be with her as she went about her daily routine.

On her first morning with us I was getting ready for school and dashed into my parents' bedroom to get something. Amah and the niece, whom I had not seen, were making up the bed. I smiled and spoke to her, with Amah translating. The niece, however, retreated to the corner of the room behind a bedpost and stared at me with wide eyes and open mouth, making not a sound.

Amah explained that I was the first Westerner she had ever seen with blond hair and a fair complexion. All her life she had heard tales of "pale people" and been warned of danger to come from such foreigners. Now she paid no heed to Amah's reassurances and, indeed, within a few days had gone happily back to their family village.

I was left to reflect upon how we Americans, with all good intentions, could not change the universal concept of us as "different." Nor could we always change the first impression of many that we might somehow be inherently dangerous and not to be trusted.

Social activities, despite the absence of some of life's finer amenities, began to reappear in the months after our return and the Shanghai way of life that once prevailed, though somewhat curbed, was making itself known again. This development applied, of course, only to our parents and other adults. Children and those in their teens—the phrase "teenager" was not yet common—were still rarely seen on any social scene.

Fashion even became important as some of the returning wives brought with them clothes from New York featuring the "New Look." This included full skirts sweeping to the ankles, providing a distinctive post-war appearance. Many an existing wardrobe then seemed outdated until Chinese tailors, quick to learn, began to copy the new styles and the fashion conscious took advantage of the opportunity to replenish their pre-war clothing supply with the latest styles.

My classmates and I were hardly fashion conscious. We had to make do with very few clothes. Western clothing of any kind still could not be purchased in any of the local department stores. Some of my friends and I were sent a few clothes by relatives in America or received hand-me-downs from friends; Jean Tucker gave me two very pretty evening dresses. At school we got along as best we could, for most of us were in the same fix—two or three skirts and sweaters had to suffice. Strangely enough the wealthy Chinese girls attending school were particularly well-dressed and always stylish, much more so than any of the rest of us.

Very few girls ever wore slacks; those who did were usually the army daughters or some of their friends, and then strictly for leisure. Chinese tailors soon began making slacks. Baggy and loose, they were most unattractive and no comparison to American-made pants; I rarely wore my one pair of these gray flannels. Shoes were a problem and most of us had only one or two pair except for summertime sandals, handmade by the Chinese. We were far from up to date in any fashion sense.

Hair styles were "natural," dependent upon bobbypins and old socks or rags (torn into strips) for any curls. In the absence of hair dryers, curling irons and accomplished stylists, hair was a constant worry to many in Shanghai's humid weather. Beyond being neat and clean, one's appearance and any extreme vanity took a back seat, in a way, to character, friendship and knowledge. It was a far different milieu for us than for our peers back in the States.

In the spring of 1948 SAS accepted the invitation of the Shanghai Jewish School to take part in one of their long-standing academic competitions. In years past our school had participated in other such events at this respected institution. Around a half-dozen similar schools would be sending four or five students to compete in what was termed a battle of the minds.

I was in the eighth grade. Each class (not the teachers) was to select one representative and those students, along with a captain, would represent SAS. I was honored to be elected by my classmates. As it turned out I was the only girl on the SAS team.

We left school on the assigned afternoon and traveled by car, with one teacher as our chaperone, the several miles down to the Hongkew district where the Jewish School, a much smaller institution, was located. Assigned a table in a crowded assembly room, we plunged at once into the quiz format.

The questions were presented orally by a moderator, with each team, after discussion among themselves, to give a written answer. At first my teammates paid me, a girl, little attention. I knew they would excel in math and science, so I said little. But when a history question was posed and the others debated in our group discussion, I spoke up. I was positive I knew the right answer. They finally agreed—and it proved to be correct. Several other questions on history and literature then fell to me and the tenth grader. Fortunately our answers were correct.

Our team placed second, a respectable and, considering the competition, even admirable standing. All of us enjoyed the experience. I, however, also learned a most valuable lesson. In these days before girls were recognized as equal to boys and when quiet deliberation did not always overcome heated discussion, I had prevailed and had, after all, contributed to the team's success. It was a lesson not to be forgotten in my future academic endeavors.

We were not in the habit of going often to the Bund. A trip to the downtown waterfront was certainly not in the same category as an American running down to the corner grocery or shopping along Main Street on a Saturday afternoon. The Bund with its huge buildings, international businesses, world-wide financial institutions and crowds of all kinds of people remained for me an area not frequently visited. But one trip to the Bund, on one hot summer afternoon, I shall never forget.

During the summer months I often spent an occasional afternoon with Annie and Sarah, two of my good friends, at Sarah's apartment. Her parents had many visitors, one of whom was a young G.I., the son of friends back in the States, recently stationed in Shanghai. At their invitation Harry made himself at home and was often at the apartment in his time off.

One afternoon when we got together we found Harry at the piano, playing one of the new songs from "South Pacific." We sat down to listen and to request some of our other favorites. He played beautifully, mostly by ear but with exquisite harmony, knowing everything from Gershwin to Berlin to the latest juke box special. He loved to play and this was a real treat for us girls. Suddenly he stopped in the middle of a song and said he had forgotten to deliver some papers connected with his duties and would have to go down to the Bund. Would we like to ride down with him?

It was almost unheard of to be asked to ride anywhere just for the ride, and with Sarah's mother's permission we each said we'd like to go. Our chauffeur wasn't coming for me for over an hour and, despite some misgivings as to what my mother might say, if Mrs. W. said it was okay, then I was going.

So we set out in his army jeep—Sarah in the front seat, Annie and I in the back, clinging to the sides of the jeep, while Harry drove with typical army abandon. I had never ridden down Avenue Joffre and Avenue Edward VII quite as fast as we now made the trip. When we reached the Bund, our speed and the obvious army jeep pushed rickshas, pedicabs, bicycles and Chinese hawkers out of our path like a tractor clearing a field. It was an August day and hot but we were going so fast that our hair actually blew in the breeze. What a reminder of America! How starved I was for such a ride!

Promising to be back in a minute, Harry pulled up in the middle of the street by one building on the Bund, grabbed a packet of papers and ran inside. There we sat, waiting for him, knowing no Chinese official would dare meddle with an army jeep, even in traffic, and knowing, too, that Harry would be back before he got into any trouble. He took only a minute or two, came running back, jumped into the seat and quickly turned the jeep around. And there we went again, speeding back up the Bund among all the traffic and throngs of people, feeling very important as we held tight to the jeep and took the curves with hair flying.

If my parents had known about this little excursion they would not have been pleased. For me, though, it was a great ride. And it remains one of my favorite memories of Shanghai and the Bund.

*O*ther special things marked those days. Going to the Chinese opera. Staying up way past midnight to hear the faint BBC broadcast of the wedding of England's Princess Elizabeth and Prince Philip. The Christmas concert by the Shanghai Symphony Orchestra. The ring of the telephone at three a.m. and a long scheduled call to Grandma Tucker in the States—well worth the three minutes for

US $25, although all we each said was "I'm fine. How are you?" Crossing the river to Pootung to see where Daddy was interned. The pajama party given by the dorm girls at the little cottage. Piano recitals in the school auditorium. A cup of tea every afternoon at four. All things not to be forgotten.

Riot at SAS

$\mathscr{T}$he spring months of 1948 were among the happiest of my stay in Shanghai. The weather was beautiful, my day to day schedule was busy and enjoyable and on the surface at least, a spirit of optimism grew around me. We had moved in March into apartment 401 at the Grosvenor House; it was much more spacious and our redecorating made it a lovely place to live. I was doing well at school; my grades were at the top and I had made some good friends, both boys and girls, boarding students and day students.

Beneath the surface of our daily life, however, the foundations of our society and the city's internal structure itself were crumbling away, bit by bit. At SAS, while we day students were more conscious of the current conditions than boarders, we were generally removed from the political events and trauma of the day. On an evening in May, though, all of us, along with our parents and other concerned Americans were jolted into an awareness of the situation around us. SAS suffered, on its campus, a demonstration and a riot.

Some of us students knew there was disagreement among the faculty and administration over the upcoming "U.N. Day." SAS had been invited to join in a city-wide celebration (something we had never done) commemorating the third anniversary of the founding of the United Nations. Each school was to prepare a program depicting their native customs, music, dances and such, which would be presented at a host school. We knew that some of the teachers questioned the wisdom of this sort of "celebration." Difficulties in transportation, language, discipline and the logistics of arranging such an assembly were valid reasons for doubt in this cosmopolitan city. Chinese schools were included and Chinese students were traditionally the source of political demonstrations that often resulted in riots; many of those involved would be older than our student body. The British school, among others, declined the invitation. The administration at SAS, however, was being pressured to cooperate and they finally agreed to participate. Everything, it seemed to some, was very loosely organized and supervised.

Our campus was chosen as a host school for part of the programs. Several lower classes, including my eighth grade, were instructed to prepare appropriate presentations. After much discussion our class decided upon an enactment of "Casey at the Bat," depicting our national pastime, baseball. I was selected by the class to be the narrator, despite my southern accent and pronunciation of the essential word "out."

There were a number of visiting classes assembled on the bleachers at our football field on the appointed day. Everything went well, with appropriate laughter and applause after each presentation. We were scheduled toward the end of the afternoon and were then all dismissed until another session began in the early evening, again on our campus.

That evening several groups assembled on the visitors' bleachers with the football field as a stage. Our bleachers held all the boarding students along with a number of day students such as myself, dutifully returning to campus to see the rest of the program. Several presentations were given, always with polite applause.

Suddenly, in a large group, the Chinese students stood, ran down the bleachers and began to build a fire on the field in front of our bleachers. More young people emerged from behind us and their group grew much larger. Some were even coming in off the street, over the bamboo wall.

They began their presentation. The main character was an older student on stilts, dressed in red and white striped pants, blue jacket and a tall red, white and blue top hat. We realized at once that this was supposed to be Uncle Sam and grew uneasy. He began tossing paper money at the Chinese seated around the fire and pointing sticks at them. Then they began stomping on an American flag lying nearby on the ground while yelling out the usual invectives against Americans. Others were pointing sticks at us in the bleachers. This was not a friendly "play."

Almost immediately Mr. Gibb, our principal, appeared at the end of the bleachers, right at my elbow. He asked if my car were there waiting for me and I nodded "Yes, sir." Then he told me to pass the word down the row that all day students were to leave immediately and go straight home. The same order went down each row.

"Now!" he said firmly.

I rose along with other day students and we started walking quickly across the campus to the front gate. Behind us we could hear Mr. Gibb's calm voice directing all the boarders to leave the field at once, go to the dorms and stay inside. Teachers present also stood and walked with the students.

The Chinese continued with their play. Behind our bleachers, still more "students" poured onto the field carrying blazing torches. They got louder and more out of control as they neared the center of the field, continuing to fill the west end of the campus, flattening and ripping apart the bamboo fence, burning grass and setting fire to parts of the bleachers. They swarmed over that end of the campus, trampling on everything in their way—and getting closer to the boys' dormitory.

The boarders reported later that all the boys, because of the spreading fire and the proximity to their dorm, were sent across campus to the first floor of the girls' dorm. All stood and watched as the demonstrators wrecked the football field and set fire to more bleachers and the bamboo fence.

Mr. Gibb and other school authorities had quickly realized that their small campus security force, made up of Chinese, could not cope with such activity and called city police for help. They were a long time coming. After two hours a few policemen arrived and finally removed the demonstrators from the campus.

All of the day students got safely home. For once the chauffeur had been told to wait for me at the school. When I got back to Grosvenor House my parents, on their way out to dinner, could not believe what I was telling them. I must be exaggerating; SAS was sacrosanct. No one would dare do such a thing. At their dinner apparently the word had not gotten out and only a few knew what was happening.

The next day, a Saturday, we all drove by the school and could see for ourselves the extensive damage and sorry appearance of our campus. A new fence was installed by Monday, the damage partially repaired and new precautionary measures taken. From then on no attention was paid to the so-called "U.N." anniversary week. Any requests for joint meetings, games, contests, etc. were turned down at once.

The authorities at SAS, chagrined at the danger brought near their students, tightened control over all of us. The surrounding Western community was stricken over the event and deeply conscious of the fact that what had happened at SAS might easily happen elsewhere. We all were learning an important lesson.

At Cathay Mansions

$\mathcal{I}$n June of 1948 my father, offered a price for our apartment he could not refuse, sold 401 Grosvenor House. We moved temporarily into a small suite of rooms at the nearby Cathay Mansions, a residence hotel in the same complex as the Grosvenor House, very British in appearance and concept. I hated to leave 401 and disliked intensely our new living quarters. We were to stay until the current volatile political situation either calmed down or escalated and we had to leave the country.

Bill quickly found a friend in a boy about his age named Miguel. Miguel was the son of a high-up government official from Venezuela. He had a Latin temperament and a head full of mischief. He pretty much had the run of the building with no restraints. In fact his various escapades so upset the management throughout the twelve floors that my parents finally forbade Bill from playing with him. By then, though, we were getting ready to move.

For me those summer weeks were filled with boredom, crowded rooms, inconvenience and little to brighten my day to day routine.

A request by Daddy, probably accompanied by a little *cumsha,* made it possible for me to practice at the grand piano that graced the hotel's eleventh floor dining room. This was open only for the evening meal so around eleven each morning, avoiding the windows that brought on my acrophobia, I slipped into the dining room and headed for the piano. I practiced my usual assignments since I was still taking weekly lessons at SAS, my teacher now another Russian, Mr. Weber. My father insisted that he was the same person who played the piano for a Shanghai dance hall band back in the '30s; this was probably true but he also played Beethoven and Mozart. Only one piece stands out for me, a reminder of that vast empty room—a "Berceuse" by Chopin. After an hour or so I left, often having glimpsed no one.

Every evening, since my parents usually escaped to the Country Club, Bill and I had our evening meal in the dining room. We ate early, under Amah's watchful eye, the only diners present. The menu reflected strong British influence. Little appealed to us but we finally began to rely upon their roast beef entrée. Every evening we ordered roast beef. For dessert only one looked good: baked Alaska. Available for two, it was a rather mundane interpretation of this elegant dessert, consisting of little beyond plain cake, bland vanilla ice cream and browned meringue. Every night we ordered baked Alaska.

On the Fourth of July our routine was pleasantly broken by the all-day gala celebration at the American Columbia Country Club. Not only was our monotonous culinary routine disrupted but there was plenty to see and do. The highlight was a magnificent display of fireworks, including one of an enormous American flag. The military band and the national anthem always brought a wave of pride and homesickness to me. It was for all of us a special day.

The routine was broken also around my birthday. Mr. Savage, one of my father's company superiors and a long-time family friend often invited for a meal, asked us to dinner at his elegant bachelor apartment. His Boy served us excellent Southern fried chicken. I was then presented with a box of one dozen white, delicately embroidered linen handkerchiefs. They were exquisitely beautiful and a cherished gift.

I remember Cathay Mansions, however, for other reasons. At the end of August a terrible typhoon blasted through Shanghai. We awoke one morning to find two or three feet of water filling the ground floor of the hotel. The main street entrance was completely closed. When elevators stopped near the lobby we were confronted with a wide expanse of dirty water stretching across the entire main floor. The only way out was to board a small sampan which ferried us across the reception area to the exterior door on Rue Cardinal Mercier. It was a shaky ride. At this smaller entrance we shifted to another small boat and were rowed up to the drier street.

Built on Shanghai's swampy marsh land, this tall brick building appeared to us to be sinking. Later we were informed that it *was* sinking—at the rate of two or three inches a year. No one seemed overly concerned. But after a day or two of this, not an unusual result of such typhoons, I was more than ever ready to move.

Fortunately the political situation had stabilized a little, or so some thought. Daddy, expecting now to remain in the city at least until spring, purchased an apartment at Cavendish Court far out Avenue Petain. It was with a sigh of relief, for several reasons, that I moved on to higher ground.

Beggar Girl

$\mathcal{T}$here she stood, this ragged Chinese beggar, her contorted, dirty face only inches from mine. I had barely closed the car window in time—her spit streaked down the glass between us. She was yelling at me, pounding on the window, her black eyes blazing, her hatred rolling over me.

We were roughly the same age, but could not have been more different. She was a Shanghai beggar, filthy in her stained, torn, dark blue padded jacket—too heavy for this warm day, but probably all the clothes she had. Born to scour the streets for her very existence, she looked cunning enough to grab whatever she could, smart enough to realize there was no escape from her sordid, dreary life. I was reflected in her eyes as blond, blue-eyed and American—well dressed, well cared for, well fed. A foreign devil.

My parents and I had been down to Yates Road shopping on this autumn afternoon. My mother was buying a few more of the exquisite hand-embroidered linens she so admired. I was more interested in items at the nearby Thieves' Market. Here we noticed three panels of a small, hand-carved Chinese screen. Once we expressed interest the shopkeeper moved quickly back into a cluttered corner and after rummaging around a few minutes came out with another five panels that completed the screen.

"Hunnert year old! Mebbe hunnert fifty!" he kept insisting.

I was particularly taken with it, as was my mother. My father began the expected bargaining procedure and after much waving of hands, raising of voices and shaking of heads by both parties, the old man finally accepted our fifth offer. Grinning, he tied up the several loose pieces into a bundle that we carried to our car.

We were on our way home when the chauffeur stopped in a long line of traffic waiting to cross a busy intersection. Spilling into the street near us were several young Chinese, loudly laughing and shouting, playfully shoving each other along the crowded sidewalk and into the gutter. Suddenly one of them, a girl, caught sight of our car—our black, two-door, nondescript, decade-old Chevrolet—and lunged toward it. Her eyes seized mine and, enraged by what she saw, her whole being seemed to erupt in violence.

Startled, I was just quick enough to roll up the back seat window beside me. Glaring at me, she began spitting at me, beating at the window with both fists, kicking the door and banging on the side of the car. Yelling and screaming at the top of her voice, she spewed out a torrent of Chinese words—words I didn't understand but whose meaning I could not mistake.

As she shook her fist in my face her companions, standing behind her, watched in amazement, glancing sheepishly at each other. She was using every weapon she had on me, in an assault without pause. I was helpless to ward off the attack and could only take the brunt of her venom, thankfully shielded by the car window. Had she been able to reach me would she have hit me? Scratched me? Clawed my eyes out?

For a second I cringed and looked away, trying to ignore her. But now I, too, was angry. I raised my chin, turned to face her and looked straight at her, my own eyes narrowing. I had a right to be here. Who was she to grind me beneath her fury? I hadn't caused her plight. I was not the reason for her misery. Nor could I ease it. Regardless of the blame she might hurl at anyone with a white, foreign—particularly American—face, I was not responsible for the squalor that surrounded her. Her own family—her own country— allowed her to live this way, had pushed her into it. Her own people condoned her wretched way of life, made her what she was.

And yet. . .

Who was I to lord it over her? Why, indeed, was I on the inside of the window?

The chauffeur glanced nervously at the intruder and her companions. As usual the car doors were locked. My father, in the front seat, and my mother, beside me, gazed stoically ahead. There was nothing they could do. There was now no "extr'ality" to protect us—no foreign police to come to our aid. Everything now was Chinese.

A few long minutes and the traffic began to move. We left her standing in the street like some raging animal, still venting her hatred. In a few months Mao Tze Tung and his Communist Party would "liberate" her along with the rest of China. If she survived until then she would no doubt be a part of the peasant army that would change the course of Chinese history. Or was she already one of them, hiding behind an ordinary facade, infiltrating the city's beggars, paving the way? Whatever her future, she would certainly demand her own full bowl of rice. Would she also give to those around her any grain of mercy?

On a hot afternoon in the fall of 1948, on a crowded Shanghai street, this young peasant woman's life touched mine for one brief, searing moment. It was a small, insignificant incident, but one long remembered. For I had glimpsed the essence of Mao's coming revolution in the seething black eyes of this Chinese beggar girl.

Warning Signs

The Shanghai that surrounded us in the fall of 1948 was a simmering cauldron of political unrest, economic disaster and social upheaval. Politically the Communists under Mao Tze Tung and the Nationalists under Chiang Kai Shek were again—or still—at war, each claiming success in his attempt to consolidate and govern the huge land mass that was China. But Mao was marching relentlessly across north-central China and Chiang was slipping noticeably farther south. Shanghai remained an entity unto itself.

The economy was shattered. The new gold yuan currency introduced that summer was going the way of other worthless Chinese money. As it sank lower in value—and it was against the law to deal in American money—prices skyrocketed. My father constantly raised the pay of the servants. There were times when he brought home their weekly wages in a cardboard carton filled with bundles of bills. Chinese money was counted in stacks of $10,000 bills folded over in packets of ten to make $100,000; ten of these, making a million, were then held together with a rubber band. A million dollars could actually purchase very little, and by the next week, even less. One Saturday he handed the whole carton, full of such bundles, over to Amah, not even dividing it. She took it back to the others who rushed out to spend its contents before its value depreciated even more.

People dealt in thousands of dollars for one loaf of bread or a handful of rice and on some days there *was* no bread and no rice. Where a bag of rice on a passing wagon had split open and trailed a few grains on the pavement, a coolie carefully swept the street and collected each grain, trying to gather something to eat.

Grainy photographs appeared in newspapers, even the foreign press, showing crowds of Chinese gathered to watch an alleged "communist" beheaded. One photo showed a "traitor" at the moment he was shot. Each meant one more "communist vermin" eliminated. Coolies pushed into these crowds, laughing and scoffing at the fate of others around them. Peasants and coolies everywhere—most uneducated, many unaware of coming change, some totally ignorant of taking political sides, others already a part of the rebelling mobs—waited for whatever the future might bring. Some Chinese students continued their work at respected institutions; others tunneled underground or disappeared into the faceless unnamed crowds, working to further Mao's cause.

Nothing was as it should be. No one knew what to expect. Foreigners seemed in limbo, waiting for something to happen. The hostility in the air was almost palpable. Americans had always been foreign devils but Westerners had once claimed protection in the foreign concessions. Now there was no such thing. The Chinese ran everything and often turned a blind eye to foreigners, particularly Americans. While many of the "missionary" Chinese remained friends to Americans, more and more Chinese were turning against us.

My family moved in September to Cavendish Court, a fairly new apartment building on Avenue Petain only two long blocks from SAS. Bill and I were elated to be so close to the school and envisioned walking back and forth, no longer dependent on the car and chauffeur. We were soon disillusioned.

More and more coolies and peasant farmers could be seen now on Petain Lu, wandering in from the nearby open countryside to form groups here and there where before there had been none. One cold afternoon I watched a small crowd staring with fascination at an old red farm tractor. Anchored on a truck bed at the side of the street, it sat alone while a young Chinese extolled its many virtues. Those around him, who had never seen or imagined such a miraculous machine, gazed at it in awe.

On an ordinary day when Bill, now nearly eleven, walked from school back home he was stopped by several Chinese boys on the sidewalk who blocked his way, refusing to let him pass. They came just short of physically attacking him, all the while letting out a stream of Chinese that Bill had no trouble translating. "Dirty American pig" and "foreign devil" usually came through clearly. He managed to get past them and ran the rest of the way home. From then on every afternoon Coolie went down the street to walk home from school with Bill. I walked home only once, extremely uneasy in the near dusk with the groups of Chinese boys huddled here and there on the sidewalk.

Other incidents occurred. Early one Saturday morning the chauffeur drove my mother and me down Avenue Joffre to a drug store not far from Grosvenor House—familiar territory. My mother had a long list of medical supplies a clerk assembled for us. My sole reason for going was to find a long desired lipstick—a tube of "Tangee," an American cosmetic for teenage girls that I was finally being allowed to use. It barely put enough color on your lips to see it, but still, in that era, it was a big addition to one's image.

When my mother and I walked back out on the street toward the car we noticed several groups of young men standing here and there on the sidewalk. There was little traffic and no policeman in sight, which was most unusual. We got into the car and the chauffeur, heading back home, stopped for a red light. At that point all of the bystanders, around twenty young men who appeared to be students, rushed toward our car. Surrounding it, they began shouting and yelling. They also began jabbering in Chinese to the chauffeur at his open window. My mother asked him what they wanted. He, almost laughing, replied that he didn't know.

At this point they began lifting and rocking the car—up and down and back and forth, all the time yelling and shouting to each other and laughing wildly. Frightened, my mother opened her purse and took out all the cash she had and handed it to the chauffeur, telling him to give it to them. Still chuckling, he pushed the bundles of cash out the window toward them, much of it falling to the street. For a few minutes the intruders paid him no attention and continued rocking the car.

Then the chauffeur gunned the engine, waved the men aside and slowly took off up the street toward home. Still no policeman had appeared. My mother was extremely upset. I was uneasy and once I thought about it, scared. She debated whether or not to tell my father, afraid he would prohibit us from going anywhere, limiting our shopping and visiting. The chauffeur, still grinning, said nothing and sped on up the nearly empty street. We looked to see if the men were following but they had dispersed. We were relieved, to say the least, when we pulled into the compound at Cavendish Court.

My mother eventually did tell my father what had happened and our activities from then on *were* limited. Rarely now did we go out of the old French Concession, except to the Country Club. I was not to walk home from school or take a pedicab but wait for the chauffeur and our car. This, coming soon after the trouble at SAS and my encounter with the angry peasant girl, unnerved all of us.

Living in Shanghai during those months became difficult and very unpleasant. We knew we were disliked and hated by many, but now we realized we might well be in actual physical danger. Warning signs abounded. We now began to heed them.

Night Watch

$\mathcal{I}$ stood at the open window of my bedroom in Cavendish Court, looking out into the evening darkness. A fine autumn mist now enveloped Avenue Petain. Below me, as I watched, another phase of Shanghai's history was ebbing away.

Only an hour or so earlier a friend and I had returned home from our Sunday night Youth Fellowship meeting at the Community Church. Few had been present and we had broken up early. As we rode back up Petain Lu I thought it odd that we saw no traffic. No car moved toward us and none followed along the wide avenue. The chauffeur drove quickly the short distance to our compound. A lone coolie and his ricksha hovered under a tree along the deserted street, then slipped around the corner at the nearby intersection. There had been rumors that the street was to be blocked off later tonight, but authorities had not specified why they were taking this unusual action and most people paid little attention.

Now below my window moved several thousand Chinese troops, a portion of Chiang Kai Shek's army stationed in Shanghai.

The pavement glistened black in the damp air while dim street lights offered only small circles of relief here and there among the shadows. I watched the lines of men stretching the breadth of Petain Lu—soldiers marching in unison under my window. In my naivete I assumed they were part of the army's defense of the city, in the process of retreat.

Rifles across their shoulders, heads bare under the threatening rain, feet keeping in step, the men marched in an ominous silence. No heavy tramp of army boots announced their presence, only the faint squeak of hundreds of flimsy tennis shoes hitting wet pavement. No shouted commands broke the quiet, only an occasional low word or two, barely audible at my window. As a street light hit their faces I saw that some were young boys. Others were obviously older, seasoned, weary troops.

Their movements almost inaudible in the chilly night air, the troops seemed—to me—engulfed in an aura of failure and stealth. This was no conquering army awaiting praise. Nor were they new recruits, lacking discipline, gathered off the city's streets and sent to fight in a glow of patriotism. According to the newspapers no battle was in the making close to the city; Mao and his communists were still well north of the Yangtze. These men appeared to be heading south and southwest. Were they moving out and leaving this city of six million to fend for itself?

In the days ahead such questions would swirl around us. How soon before Mao would reach Shanghai? How many of these troops would stay with Chiang? How many desert to home villages and then slip into Mao's shining promises?

I understood that whatever defense of the city lay ahead, certainly it would take many more troops than these and many more supplies. Or was Shanghai not to be defended at all? Would it simply be left to its own fate?

The collapse of the economy and the attitude of Chiang and his Nationalist Party led many a Westerner to question their actions and to wonder if the time had come once again to close businesses and evacuate families. To leave China to wrestle alone with her destiny. The threat of another war was enough to drive most Americans out of the country. Or was Mao, as some insisted, to become a blessing, and welcome foreign business and foreign money?

The mist and fog had turned into a steady autumn rain. The troops continued their silent march toward the city limits and the waiting countryside. On toward an uncertain future.

I glanced up the street and could see only more soldiers marching toward me. It was getting late so I turned and got into bed. For a long time the muffled *swish-squeak* of hundreds of rain-soaked tennis shoes still sounded beneath my window.

Shanghai, Shangbie

$\mathcal{T}$he evacuation order from the American Consular-General was announced over the radio late in the afternoon on a day in early November. Letters soon would arrive for all American citizens informing them of the order. I was visiting a friend who lived several floors above us; I quickly ran back down to our apartment. It was the same message I had heard before: all Americans were to leave China as soon as possible.

Three weeks later I came home from school, walked into my bedroom and stared in anguish at the two suitcases and small army locker piled in the middle of the floor. Not again. This would be the third time in my fourteen years that I would be forced to drastically change my life because of conditions over which I, and even my parents, had no control. Something deep inside me was screaming at having once more to pack my belongings and leave home, a familiar routine, school and friends. People I held dear. I would not go! Except that I had no choice.

I caught my own eyes in the mirror before me and without

thinking the words poured angrily out of me. Someday. Someday! Whenever all this was over and done with—and it couldn't last forever—I would find a safe place in the middle of America. I would settle down—permanently. Never, ever would I leave or move again.

But I was very much aware of the danger around me. Mao Tze Tung was more than simply a name in the newspaper. We knew there would be trouble ahead, sooner rather than later. I did not need the U.S. State Department to tell me it was time to go.

At least this time my father was going with us. He would get us settled somewhere in the States and then he would return to Shanghai, Tsingtao and Manila, to work for the company two years or so until he could retire. But what about me? Where were we going? Toward what future?

I turned to the task at hand. The tears did not flow; I had been told years ago not to cry. Necessity and anger took over. Gathering up my things, I opened the suitcase.

Our way out this time would be not via an ocean luxury liner. Few such ships now sailed the Orient, stopping at this port-of-call. We would go instead by a Pan American Airways plane. Arrangements had been made. We were scheduled to leave on December 7 at seven o'clock in the evening.

In the few remaining days the BAT sent coolies in to pack most of our furniture and household goods which would follow by freighter, along with some of our clothes and personal items. We could carry with us one suitcase each. Some of our belongings we were giving away, others we were selling. My mother sold her Singer sewing machine for twenty-five dollars US to the wife of one of the assistants at the factory. Our faithful old Chevrolet Daddy sold to someone else at the factory for seven hundred US—twice what

Mama had paid for it in 1941. The apartment we simply walked away from, losing all of the purchase price.

We had already told many friends goodbye. Some left Shanghai almost immediately—flights were filled with families leaving for the States. Some left with little warning; one day they were just gone. Others were determined to wait it out. Things, they thought, might not be that bad; they would wait and see.

One evening Annie invited eight friends, both boys and girls, to a dinner for me at Sun Ya's, *the* Shanghai restaurant for Chinese food. We ate upstairs in the reserved area, with special service, at a big round table. It was a lovely evening.

The rolls at school were every day growing shorter and shorter as one by one students withdrew. Classes, though much diminished in size, continued as usual. I kept going until the last day, loath to leave these special people.

On the final morning Bill and I went on to school as usual, knowing the chauffeur would be returning around eleven to take us home. It was not easy telling these friends goodbye. One girl was in the infirmary so I went outside and around behind the building to her window to wave at her. Annie was the hardest; I knew that I would probably never see her again.

Once back at the apartment we watched our servants assemble on the front steps of the building to have their picture taken. We then went down the line speaking to each one, telling each goodbye. I got to Amah and my heart stopped. What would happen to this frail little woman when Mao took over? Would she be safe, even back in her own village? And Coolie—so smart and capable, with so much to offer and so much of life ahead of him; where would he fit into Mao's plans? My thanks to them were hard to express through tears. But I think they understood.

A company chauffeur and car now took us out to the Country Club. There we would eat lunch, while away the long afternoon and make a pretense of eating an early supper. Finally we headed out to the Hungjao Airport.

Several close friends joined us at the airport. One other BAT wife was scheduled on our flight, a young woman and good friend who had grown up in China and now was leaving her American husband behind again—she had been evacuated in 1940 with us and he had been interned with my father.

The lounge, dimly lit, was a small bare cement area with only a few benches to sit on. One of Daddy's friends had brought paper cups and a much appreciated bottle of bourbon with him to wish us bon voyage; all the adults promptly shared it with thanks. Bill and I had no such solace.

My father was particularly concerned about cash he wanted to take with us—some seven hundred dollars of U.S. money. It was against Chinese law to have any American money in your possession. The problem was how to get it, an enormous amount in those days, out of the country. There was no time to move it through the bank and besides, it would be needed on our trip. He had put the entire amount inside his sock and shoe—and walked very carefully. We had no idea whether our luggage would be searched or if we would be inspected before leaving the country; thankfully we were not and escaped any trouble in that area. As soon as we had taken off, Daddy removed his sock and shoe—and the money—with relief.

None of us except my father had ever flown and we were nervous. It helped a little to remember that we had no other way out; it was beyond our control. This was it. One of the Chinese running the airport came over and told Daddy it was time to board the plane so we exited the lounge for the cold dark night. Few lights marked the way out to the runway where the enormous Pan American clipper sat waiting.

We settled into our assigned seats. Nervous as we were it did not help our frame of mind to hear the news, passed down the aisle, that this pilot was flying "blind" for the first time and would be taking off and then landing in Tokyo only by instruments—a dangerous procedure to our ears, or so it seemed at the time. I could hear the engines being revved up and then felt the plane move down the runway.

In the dark we could see little that looked familiar. Flying low, the pilot circled the city. Below me I could see lights I knew were in the French Concession, where Grosvenor House and S.A.S., Amah and Annie were. We could easily make out the brightly lit Bund and a stream of cars, as well as a few ships on the Whangpoo and the Yangtze. Then came the darkness of the ocean.

Shanghai. Shangbie.

Shanghai. Farewell, with sadness.

Epilogue: Journey Home

$\mathcal{W}$e landed safely, despite the radar, or perhaps because of it, touching down at the Tokyo airport at some hour after midnight. Buses were waiting to carry us to our overnight accommodations. We rode past blocks and blocks of bombed out, desolate areas, winding up on the outskirts of the city at its huge deserted railroad yards. Off to one side, alone on one of the tracks, were three pullman cars where the buses stopped. We were led to our assigned compartments—Mama and I had one and next to us, Daddy and Bill. Modern appliances greeted us along with the typical pullman berths. It was eerily quiet, with few lights anywhere around us. I got little sleep.

The next morning at eight the buses pulled up, we got on and were driven to the Tokyo Hotel for breakfast. After a scant meal we took off again for a ride around Tokyo and a long visit at the National Museum of Japan, a large building well cared for and offering a wide variety of beautiful exhibits and historical items.

Back on the bus we took another long ride which included a glimpse of General Douglas MacArthur's hat as he entered his headquarters, surrounded by people. Back at the hotel we had our scheduled lunch and then boarded the bus again for the airport and another plane to continue our flight.

Our next stop was Wake Island. It was the middle of the night and all I saw was a large Quonset hut where we wandered around while the plane refueled. Sometime in the next few hours we passed the International Date Line and gained a day—we assumed it was December 8 again.

From there we flew to Midway Island. It was now broad daylight but the hours were beginning to blur. Our interest here was in the "looney birds" who flocked along the beach and did their special dance for us.

The next stop was Hawaii, then a U.S. territory. Now in the dark again, we landed at Honolulu's airport. I emerged from the plane and could do nothing but stand and breathe in the heavenly, flower-scented air.

Thank God for America!

We stayed a week at the Moana Hotel in Honolulu, playing in the water at Waikiki Beach, lunching at the Royal Hawaiian Hotel, standing in awe at Pearl Harbor, admiring Diamond Head and finally waving goodby as we passed the Aloha Tower.

We sailed for the mainland on the *SS Lurline,* a magnificent luxury liner heading for California. Five days later, passing Alcatraz and the Golden Gate Bridge, we docked at the pier in San Francisco. We registered at the St. Francis Hotel, staying for only a few days but seeing, among other sights, the cable cars and our first television program.

We then boarded an express train for the east coast, traveling across the Great Salt Lake, the Rockies, middle America and the Appalachians to Virginia and down to Richmond. Here we caught local number three for La Crosse. We pulled into the station around three in the afternoon, right on time.

It was Christmas Eve, 1948. After nearly fifteen years, my China odyssey was over. This part of my life was ending.

My ricksha days, once reality, now settled into memory.

Shanghai, 1947

We were among the first of the BAT families to return to Shanghai after the war and our apartment was among the first to be restored to a semblance of its prewar comfort.

. . .We had moved . . . into apartment 401 at the Grosvenor House; it was much more spacious and our redecorating made it a lovely place to live.

GROSVENOR HOUSE
AND
GROSVENOR GARDENS

RUE CARDINAL MERCIER
(OPPOSITE CERCLE SPORTIF FRANCAIS)

MODERN APARTMENTS

DISTI   OPS

TO
REC   73874
THE   1430

. . . My father immediately contacted the principal's office to enroll my brother and me in the third and seventh grades . . .

. . . there was something special about the Shanghai American School. . . . With its colonial architecture, red brick Georgian buildings with white trim, and wide green lawns the school seemed a bit of America set down on this foreign soil, offering all of us a little piece of home.

SEVENTH GRADE

Photo courtesy 1947 Columbian

FIRST ROW
(Standing)

Helga Muell... ...tel, Leta Mae Tucker,
Ann

Fred

Marga...

Photo courtesy 1949 Columbian

My name had somehow been misspelled in the main office—
with an "e" for May—and despite specific requests and
numerous explanations to teachers with their roll books, it
never seemed to get corrected.

Report cards came out twice a semester. They were not given
to us, but mailed to our parents at home.

SHANGHAI AMERICAN SCHOOL
10 HENG SHAN LU

Shanghai American School
High School
Periodic Scholastic Report

Report of __Leta Mae Tucker__ 8
at the end of the __5th__ week
of the school year. __1947-48__

Date: October 21, 1947.

Course	Grade	Comments
English	97	Leta Mae takes up each project and perfects herself in it. To stay where she is, however, she must catch on very quickly from now on.
Mathematics	98	Leta Mae prepares her mathematics assignments perfectly and makes valuable contributions to the class by her thoughtful questions.
Science	94	Leta Mae is well mannered and attentive in class. Her preparations are thorough and well thought out.
Music	A	
Social Studies	95	Excellent in preparation and recitation.

Thomas C. Gibb
Principal

At each report period, students are graded according to a cumulative percentage system. The passing grade for any course is 65%. An examination in each course is administered at the end of the 18th and 34th weeks of the school year and, while the grades are reported at that time, they are not averaged with the cumulative grades of the student.

No pupil will be promoted unless his cumulative grades for all courses undertaken during the year are passing even though he passes examinations in all of his courses.

Comments by the teacher, edited by the Principal, usually described the pupil's attitude and application in the effort required for the course.

Parents are urged to communicate with the school if there is anything in this report upon which they wish to comment and if they feel that they can supply additional information in regard to the studies of the student.

My favorite [thirteenth birthday gift] was a delicate sandal-wood Chinese fan, decorated with flowers on a green background. It looked and smelled so delicious.

I shall always remember her [Ann] fondly . . . because of a special gift she gave me for Christmas . . . a set of four small porcelain T'ang Dynasty horses . . .

. . . we noticed three panels of a small, hand-carved Chinese screen. Once we expressed interest the shopkeeper moved quickly back into a cluttered corner and after rummaging around a few minutes came out with another five panels that completed the screen.

I practiced my usual assignments since I was still taking weekly lessons at SAS, my teacher now another Russian, Mr. Weber.

To play Chopin became a goal most desirable and not, I thought, impossible.

. . . I was honored to be elected by my classmates. As it turned out I was the only girl on the SAS team. . . . Assigned a table in a crowded assembly room, we plunged at once into the quiz format.

Photo courtesy
1948 Columbian

Tucker & A. Walline Star
Weber's 3rd Piano Recital
iven At School On Nov. 21

**r. Weber Plays Two Duets
ith A. Overholt and B. Barr**

On Sunday afternoon, Nov-
mber 21, Mr. Weber gave his
rst recital this year in the
chool auditorium. Eleven of
is best pupils performed for a
mall but appreciative audience,
nd they all did very well.

The stage was decorated,
with potted plants and large
white bunches of chrysanthe-
nums. The curtain rose at
3:15, and Mr. Owens gave a
short welcoming speech. First
on the program was Betty
Brewster, who played Rubin-
stein's "Melody in F". Later
Abbie Overholt and Mr. Weber
played two Hungarian Dances
and Mary Newman finished the
first part of the program with
"Humoresque" by Rachmaninoff.

There was an intermission of
ten minutes before Part II of
the recital began. The more
advanced students played in
this half, and Abbie Overholt
began with Chopin's "Valse in
E Minor". Other highlights of
th program were Kathy Oltman
playing "Claire de Lune", Liszl's
"Dream of Love" played by
Betty Jean Rugh, Grieg's "Wedding March" played by Betty
Barr, and Leta Mae Tucker
played "Etude" by Chopin. Mr.
Weber and Betty Barr also
played two Spanish Dances by
Moskowsky as duets. Then
bringing the recital to an impressive close, Anne Walline
presented Liszt's "Rigoletto" and
"Polonaise in Ab Major" by
Chopin.

PART I	
...s Kepler	Fr. Schubert
	J. Massenet
...Stannard	C. Chaminade
...opin's 1st mov.	L. V. Beethoven
David Bridgman	
Rondo Capricio	F. Mendelsohn
Joyce Kirichek	
Prelude in C sharp min	S. Rachmaninoff
Abbie Overholt	
Gavotte Miniature	M. H. Brown
Two piano duet sp. arr.	M. H. Brown
PART II	
Fantasie Impromptu in C sharp min	Fr. Chopin
Mary Newman	
Andante Cantabile from Sonata	
"Pathetique"	L. V. Beethoven
Ruth Koeppe	
Consolation in D Flat	Fr. Liszt
Invitation to the Dance	C. M. von Weber
Betty Barr	
Polichinelle op 3 N. 4	S. Rachmaninoff
Aberesque	Cl. Debussy
Betty Jean Rugh	
Gardens	Eastwolin
De Bostman	D. Smith
Ave Maria	Arcadelt
Though Philomela Lost Her Love	Thomas Morley
Glee Club	
PART III	
Humoresque	A. Dvorak
In Gondola	Fr. Bender
Two Pianos duet sp. arr	H. M. Brown
Leta Mae Tucker	
Betty Jean Rugh	
Warsaw Concerto	Rich. Addinsell
Leta Mae Tucker	
Concerto in A min	Ed Grieg
Anne Walline	
Two pianos duets, Second piano	A. Weber
Heire Kati op. 32 N. 4	Jeno Hubay
Nocturne op. 9 N. 2	Fr. Chopin
Schoen Rosmarin	Fr. Kreisler
Violin Solo	
Mr. St. Hartmann-Balasa	
At the piano—A. Weber	

FRIDAY, MARCH 19, 1948

SAS Places Second In Quiz At JCC

On Monday 8th a Quiz Centest
took place at the Jewish Community Center. Six schools including S.A.S. participated. Each
team had five "Quiz Kids" whose
ages ranged from twelve to
fifteen years. The S.A.S. Quiz
team was as follows:

10th grade Bruce Roberts
(captain)
Ben. Gilson
9th Grade Thomas Kepler
8th grade Leta Mae Tucker
7th grade David Abell

The other contestants represented the Jewish Schools.

Each team sat at a separate
table from the others in the
"Quiz Room" (the lounge of the
Community Center.) Forty questions were asked by the quizmaster. These questions were
taken from the following subjects:

Art and Literature
Brain Twisters
Geography
History
Science
Sports

After reading each question
the quizmaster allotted a certain
amount of time for answering
it (a half, one, two or three
minutes). When the allotted,
time for answering a question
was up, all answers were passed
to the jury of whom Mrs. Barr
was one. The jury then made
their decisions. Answers counted from one to three points de-
pending on the type of question.
Each team was allowed to discuss within itself every question
asked before handing the answer
in to the jury. Answers blanks
or forms were provided for each
team.

The first two terms held their
positions from the very beginning of the contest right
through to the end. The winner
was the Shanghai Jewish Youth
Association with forty-six and
a half points. The second place
was taken by S.A.S. with forty-
three points.

A million dollars could actually purchase very little, and by the next week, even less.

Chinese money was counted in stacks of $10,000 bills folded over in packets of ten to make $100,000; ten of these, making a million, were then held together with a rubber band.

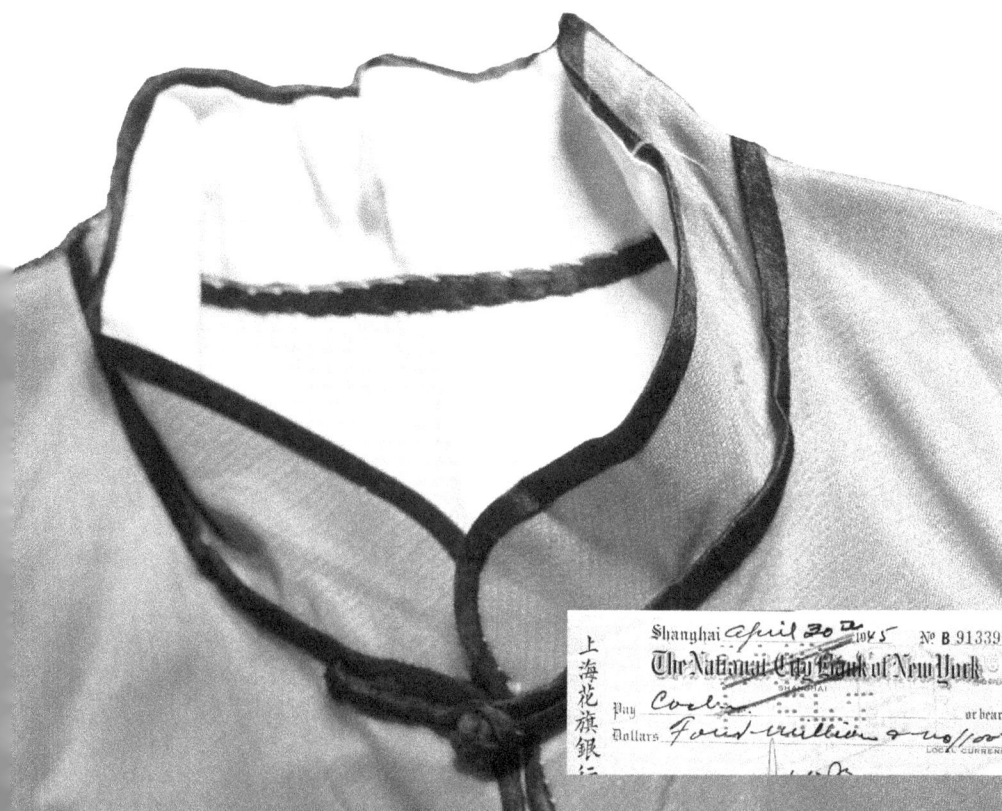

. . . The rolls at school were every day growing shorter and shorter as one by one students withdrew.

More S.A.S. Students Leaving For States

More and more students have been leaving S.A.S., and some are still planning to go. The school is sorry to see them leave, but is trying to carry on as best as it can.

Mary and Jean Kepler left on Dec. 4 on the General Anderson. The ship is bound for San-Francisco. When they arrive, they plan to go to San Diego for a few weeks, and then leave for the East. They didn't want to leave as they had been here for two and a half years and had made many friends. Jean said that she would miss German class and Malory Torrey, while Mary would weep most tears over Geometry, Miss Plaum and Henry Glucker.

Also on the General Anderson were Jimmy and Caroline Ware bound for Tupelo, Mississippi. Jimmy definitely did not want to leave, as he will miss Betty and all the rest of his honorable associates. Caroline wanted to go, but plans to come back after college. Both of them will go to Tupelo High where they were before they came to S.A.S.

Leta Mae Tucker left for Honolulu on Dec. 7 at 7 p.m. on a Pan American Plane. She planned to stay in Honolulu for four or five days, and then go en route to San Francisco. She will probably live outside Richmond, Virginia, where she will be right at home with that Southern accent. She did not want to leave S.A.S. and will miss Glee Club and playing the piano for the kids. She is anxious to get back to Virginia, however, and see her family and friends again.

Another departure was that of Sarah Workman who left by plane for Manila on Dec. 9. She was very thrilled over the trip, because it would be the first time she had ever been, in a plane. Her family went to Manila because they want to stay fairly near China so that if it will be easy to get back later on. Sarah did not want to leave all her friends and the teachers, and she said that she would miss writing articles for the Sh'Am!

Fussy Styles, a post graduate, was the next one to go, leaving Dec. 17 on a Pan American Plane today headed for Washington D.C. She will miss, and will be missed in Hockey. She plans to stay in Washington for two months and then go with her parents to some other country where her father will be transferred. She will return to the States and go to college next fall.

A large group are leaving Dec. 27 on the Breckenridge, a navy transport. Among them are Sarah Alice and Mary Francis Fenn, two well beloved boarders. They plan to go to Princeton in the States and then on to Geneva, Switzerland. Sarah Alice will come back to the States for her Senior year. Both of them will miss their room-mates, while Mary Fran will especially miss the strenuous hockey practices, and Sarah Alice staying up late listening to the radio.

Bruce Roberts, who is bound for Massachusetts where he lived formerly, is also leaving on the Breckenridge. He is one of the few who wants to go, but he admits that he will miss the friendliness and all the kids here.

(Continued on page 10, col

'49

COLUMBIAN

. . . China shadowed my life, influenced my character, . . . and settled into a corner of my heart.

About the Author

Leta May Tucker Hodge was born in 1934 in Tientsin, China where her father was in the tobacco business. Her childhood years were spent in Shanghai and in La Crosse and Chester, Virginia where she graduated from high school in 1952.

She attended Westhampton College, University of Richmond, graduating Phi Beta Kappa in 1956 with a B.A. degree. After teaching in high school for three years she returned to academic pursuits, in 1959 receiving a Woodrow Wilson National Fellowship and the following year a Thomas Jefferson Fellowship for graduate study in history at the University of Virginia.

In 1961 she married Edward D. Hodge and moved to Mexico, Missouri where he practiced law. They are the parents of three daughters and have five grandchildren.

She served as director of the Audrain County Historical Society and Museum from 1980 until 1990. She has written extensively on local history.

www.ingramcontent.com/pod-product-compliance
Lightning Source LLC
Chambersburg PA
CBHW062043080426
42734CB00012B/2548